THE SECOND PROMISE

*AN INTENSELY MOVING,
HEART GRIPPING AUTOBIOGRAPHY
THAT REVEALS THE ANGUISH,
LONELINESS, COURAGE & FEARS*

*OF ONE MAN'S JOURNEY
THROUGH BOOT CAMP,
VIETNAM'S JUNGLE WAR
& RETURNING HOME
...REACHING BACK
TO TOUCH & HEAL*

JACK D. ADAMS

This is Book 516 out of 750
Jack D. Adams
4/20/99

Sale of this book without a front cover may be unauthorized. If this book is missing its cover, it may have been reported to the publisher as "unsold or destroyed" and neither the author nor the publisher may have received payment for it.

Published by Iron Star
P.O. Box 282
Carthage, Tennessee 37030
The Second Promise: Copyright © 1999 by Jack D. Adams
First Printing 1999

All rights reserved. Except for use in review, no portion of this book may be reproduced in any form without the express written permission of the publisher.

Cover Design and Photographs by Kirby Allen
Illustration by Neil Logan

FIRST EDITION

Library of Congress Catalog Card Number: 99-94271

ISBN: 0-7392-0174-3

Printed in the USA by

MORRIS PUBLISHING

3212 East Highway 30 • Kearney, NE 68847 • 1-800-650-7888

DEDICATION

To the 58,000 fighting men who died in Vietnam
and whose names are etched on the great *Wall*
in Washington DC.

To all the missing in action and their families.

To the one hundred plus Canadian veterans who died
while serving in our battles during Vietnam,
and to their wounded..... many I knew
and still know on a personal level.

To the POW's returned and those remaining there.

To the disabled veterans.

To the Vietnam veterans and their families,
for whom this book was conceived.

CONTENTS

ACKNOWLEDGMENTS .... *xi*

PART I : INTRODUCTION

THE PROMISE .... *xv*
FOREWORD .... *xvi*

PART II : BOOT CAMP

THE CHOICE 2
BOOT CAMP 2
OLD WARRIORS NEVER CRY 3
GENERAL ORDERS 4
BAYONET 5
THE 45 5
KILL, KILL, KILL 6
RIFLE-M14 6
LEARN WELL 7
THE TITLE 8
THIRTY DAY LEAVE 9

PART III : VIETNAM

TRAINED 11
THOUGHTS ABOUT NAM 11
WELCOME TO NAM 12
THIS STRANGE LAND VIETNAM 12
NEW HOME 13
YOUR GEAR 13
NEW GUY 14
TWELVE MONTHS 15
CLEAN RIFLE 15

CONTENTS

HOW MUCH LONGER	16
TO RULE	17
ENVISIONED WAR	18
FIRST PRAYER	19
THE HEAT	20
DIG IN	20
BOUNCING BETTY	21
DEADLY PREMONITION	22
MY FRIEND	23
MY BUNKER	24
YOUR SON, MY FRIEND	25
SWAMP WATER	26
BLACK TAPED EDGE	26
CAM LO	27
HEAR WHAT I SEE	28
THE NEXT ROUND	29
NO MORE NICE GUY	30
DOOR GUNNER	31
REVENGE	32
A LITTLE REST	32
ONE ROUND	33
HIDE & SEEK NAM STYLE	33
DEATH AWAITS	34
GRAVE RATS	35
COFFEE NAM STYLE	36
THE PONCHO	36
TRADE OUT MY M-14	37
CLAYMORE	38
LIE AND WAIT	38
THE CORPSMAN	39
DUST OFF	39
NO RICH KIDS	40
IF IT MOVES	41
NEW NAME	41
MIND RAPE	42

CONTENTS

QUESTIONS, WHAT ANSWERS	42
THE MARINES ARE COMING	43
LETTER TO A WARRIOR	44
VIETNAM AND COUNTING	45
READY YOURSELF	45
THE LATRINE SCENE	46
TUNNEL RAT	47
CHRISTMAS IN VIETNAM	48
B-52 FLY BY	49
NAPALM	49
VIETNAM SHAKES	50
BEATING CHARLIE	51
MONSOON RAIN	51
LETTER HOME TO DAD	52
DEAR JOHN	52
INCOMING	53
BAD NEWS	54
MISTAKES	55
BAMBOO POLES	55
EYES	56
M-79 BLOOPER	57
NO SCREAMING IN THE DARK	58
THE VISIT	58
GOD IS NOT WITH THE MEN IN VIETNAM	59
LETTER HOME TO MOM	60
JUNGLE ROT	61
SHORT TIMER	62
SEARCH THEN DESTROY	63
KIDS ARE KIDS	64
NO SLACK AT ALL	65
SPIDER HOLE	65
NO BETTER WAY	66
DEATH	66
HOW COME	67
CHARLIE'S LAST CHANCE	68

CONTENTS

LAUGHING AND DYING...68
SQUAD LEADER..69
TRICK WE TRIED..70
HOW DID IT FEEL TO KILL (YOU ASKED).................71

PART IV : RETURNING HOME

WELCOME HOME...73
RE-UP...74
HOME AGAIN, BIG DEAL..75
THE KID BACK HOME...76
INTERVIEWS...77
BATTLES REAL REWARDS..77
DON'T LISTEN..78
DON'T MEAN MUCH..78
WAR..79
SILENT WARRIORS...80
I DON'T CARE..80
REMEMBERING...81
PHONE CALLS...82
SATISFIED (THE BIGGER THEY ARE).......................83
NEVER THE SAME..84
EMOTIONS AND FEELINGS..84
LOST FEELINGS, LOST FRIEND................................85
VETERANS' DAY...86
VIETNAM VET'S TIDE...87
THE MIND..88
GUILT...89
DARK AND DEEP...89
FORGETTING WAR...90
THE NEED...91
MY HANDS..92
WON IN WAR..92
EXPLAIN TO HER..93
A POEM I WOULD HAVE LIKED TO RECEIVE..........94

CONTENTS

JULY FOURTH FLASHBACKS	95
DAMN DREAMS	96
TO SLEEP NOT DREAM	97
HEY, GOD	98
THE DAYMARE	99
NAM VET FEELING BAD	99
SILVER STAR	100
THE SERVICE	101
GOOD-BYE	102
COMBAT VET	102
HAPPY TO SEE YOU	103
CONSCIENCE	104
JUDGMENT DAY	105
NIGHTMARES OF VIETNAM	106
WHAT WOULD THEY SAY	107
CHILD OF DREAD	108
BIG WORDS	109
PUSH COMES TO SHOVE	110
HELL'S OWN DREAM	111
WHO WILL I MEET TONIGHT	112
URGE TO KILL	112
NEVER HEAL	113
GETTING LATE	114
ANY IDEA	115
THE HOUR	116
MASTER DREAMER	117
ONE YEAR LATER	118
APOLOGIES	119
JUNKIE HOOKED ON WAR	120
THE TATTOO ARTIST	126
STANDARD ANSWERS	128
DISABLED	129
THE MORNING	130
PSYCHE WARD	131
PREMATURE DEATH	132

CONTENTS

NAM WAS A CHESSBOARD..133
SORROW...133
FREEDOM TO SING..134
THE NIGHT...135
IT WILL HEAL...136

PART V : REMEMBERING....BROTHERS & SISTERS

THE WALL...138
WHAT CAN I SAY..139
THE CONFLICT...139
OPERATION FREEDOM BIRD.....................................140
NURSES MEMORIAL STATUE....................................141

PART VI : YOU ARE NOT ALONE

YOUR JOURNEY BACK TO LIFE.................................143
HELPING YOURSELF...144
COMBAT HISTORY..150

GLOSSARY...152

ACKNOWLEDGMENTS

I wish to thank my family.... Mom, Dad, Bob, Kevin, and Blaine, for standing by me even though they couldn't understand what thirteen months of killing, death and dying does to a person; and for loving me when I was most unlovable. They lost their son and brother.... I returned home an animal, yet, they never gave up on me.

To John Reyna Tapia of Prescott, Arizona. Thank you for serving in W.W.II... wounded three times, Korea... wounded four times. I have never seen so many well deserving medals, including seven Purple Hearts. Your devotion to our country and all you continue to do for veterans, goes without question. Thanks for your encouragement in so much of my life. Most of all, thanks for being the best friend a guy could have.

Thanks to Marty Martin, a brother, friend and fellow combat veteran.

Thanks to Neil Logan for his talent and dedication in creating the statue; and especially for enabling me to keep my first promise.

To Ken Hall, Team Leader of the Outreach Vet Center in Prescott, Arizona. A very special thanks for all the help you have given me, and for your dedication in helping all of us.

To Ted Rea, for the talks we've had; and for the very special olive branch which holds a great deal of meaning to me.

To U.S. Senator John McCain, and his staff assistant Tom McCanna, for all your help....not only to me, but to the many veterans I know you've helped over the years. Your support gave me what was needed to keep going on.

To the United States Marine Corps, and the Department of the Army for providing me with information I needed along the way.

My undying thanks to William Gooding Jr., a fellow warrior, and my brother, who's name appears throughout the book. He was there with me and knows the reality behind the words I write. We both made it back!

A SPECIAL THANKS

To all those who helped with the making of this book.
Without your help, this would never have been possible...

Kirby, my soul mate, my best friend... For your love,
endless devotion, and believing in me like no other. For the
months you spent typing to get it back into the original format.
For the care you took creating the page layout, and cover design.
For finding such a great company .....Morris Publishing,
making phone calls, and handling every little detail.
You are the one who pulled it all together

To your mom, Veronica, for the hours spent proofreading.

To Marilyn Saeger of Prescott, Arizona
for your caring of Veterans, and for all that you do
to help everyone, including me.

To all those who helped fulfill my first promise
by getting the Memorial Statue placed in Prescott, Arizona.

To all those who helped with the
"*Tribute to Veteran Display*," including all
dignitaries and celebrities who cared enough to respond,
letting us know ....we are not forgotten.

To TCWR records who gave veterans their first
"*Veteran Tribute Album*," <u>These Colors Won't Run</u>,
and allowing me to become a small part of the project.
I remember my first order to 1-888-OUR VETS,
and hope you receive calls for years to come.

PART I

INTRODUCTION

THE PROMISE

A promise was made, back in 1985
That Prescott would honor
Those who fought and those who died.

There was W.W.I and W.W.II
Our veterans responded
And fought for the red, white and blue.

Then came Korea, followed by Vietnam
Again our warriors fought
To protect the freedom of this great land.

No greater sacrifice could have been made
No greater price could have been paid
By those served and the names you'll find engraved

They faced the blood and gore on battlefields of red
They saw the badly wounded and the faces of the dead.
Gallantly they stood, for they had a job to do
Fearlessly they fought for the red, white and blue.

Some fought on while others died.
Now, Prescott honors you, by showing you our pride.
Now, is the time to release the tears
That some have held back for years.

Let us take a minute and say a silent prayer
For those who died, those who returned,
And the ones remaining there.

Jack D. Adams

FOREWORD

Warriors have survived war and returned from battles even before records of man's existence were kept. There is little question that the events of combat have always left their indelible, psychological stigma upon their participants.

Fear, pain, isolation, excitement and years of emotional turmoil have most certainly been part of the lot of all men and women. While the state of the art of assisting and treating the short and long term emotional sequelae of combat has been greatly advanced as a result of the Vietnam War, it is important to note that the Vietnam veteran, particularly the combat veteran, is a unique and special entity---in many ways different from any other such group in history---and that the Vietnam War itself was quite unlike any other.

The Vietnam Conflict holds the record as the longest and most economically costly war ever fought by the United States. The destructive power unleashed by this country alone far exceeds that of all the combatants of World War II. It is also factual (to the detriment of all citizenry) that it was the most profoundly unpopular war in this country's history.

Memories of anti-war demonstrations and widespread popular lack of support for the war are still fresh for most of us. While it is true that most protesters were motivated to protect the interest of our citizens and servicemen involved in the war, it is also true that the tremendous nationwide unpopularity of the war had numerous long-lasting effects on our country and it's population, particularly those who in any way participated in Vietnam.

The sense of betrayal, anger, isolation, and lack of acknowledgment frequently expressed by many Vietnam veterans should come as no surprise. Many often felt and still feel that their own government had lied to them, and that their resentment is often expressed about being set apart and different and about being a minority, which they certainly are.

It is the sad truth that after doing their DUTY in Asia, they did not come home to the thanks, parades, pretty girls, and hoopla which almost traditionally would mark such events. They came home to embarrassed silence and uneasiness in others.

It is also true that even within our traditional veterans organizations, many Vietnam veterans often felt isolated, different, and looked down upon. This is being written in 1985, some ten years after the inglorious finale of out involvement in Vietnam, and in a real sense, many of our veterans of the war have not yet truly come home.

Jack Adams' poetry represents a painful, honest tribute to himself and to all fellow veterans of the conflict. His use of writing of poetry to help heal is evident. His results are sensitive and touching. His encouragement of others to travel a similar path is excellent advise for many.

His recommendations to search for good support is also of great potential value. To be on such a venture by oneself is unthinkable. Jack's poetry and this book is also intended for the non-warrior, non-veteran. The most passive of individuals cannot help but be moved by the realities that LEAP from each verse.

For some it may be difficult at times to continue reading without stopping for a while. It was for me. I know Jack Adams, and I know that he writes the truth.

His truths are neither pretty nor easy to digest, yet it is the truth, and thus at the very least deserves attention. Also, let us not forget that, like it or not, as Americans, we dispatched Jack and his comrades for their mission. I believe that we owe Jack and all the rest of them at least an attentive audience. If this book doesn't help convince that we should reflect a bit before we enter the next war, it is at least my hope that, in some small way it might help us all deal with that part of the inevitable aftermath of war that the warriors bring home with them.

    Dr. Paul Zeltzer, M.D.
        Former Acting Chief of
        Psychiatry
        Fort Whipple Veterans Hospital
        Prescott, Arizona 86313

AUTHOR'S NOTE

I made a lot of promises in the bush, in hopes that God would help me make it home alive. I have done my best to keep these promises. The first promise I made to myself: I wanted to have a memorial in the town where I lived to remind people of the guys that were killed in Vietnam..... my friends and all the others. When I got out of the Marines in 1968, it was all I could do to survive day-to-day. Forgetting was my priority. But twenty one years later, that promise began haunting me.

In 1985 I met a sculpture, Neil Logan, who had just finished a memorial in Texas. A fellow veteran, Marty Martin, made the introduction. We sat down to talk, and that's when the memorial became a reality. Marty and I posed for the statue, he is the standing soldier and I am the wounded soldier. In April, 1989 the memorial titled "*Medivac/Dust-off,*" was dedicated and placed in the town square of Prescott, Arizona.

I also made another promise.... if I made it back, I would let people know what the war was really like, in hopes there will never be another. With help and encouragement along the way, I now give you the *Second Promise*..........

PART II

BOOT CAMP

THE CHOICE

I received a letter from Uncle Sam
Informing me I'm not a free man.
I was told to report at a place in L.A.
And be prepared to stay all day.

The letter said if I don't report
There were measures that would resort.
As an American it's my duty to fight,
It doesn't matter if it's wrong or right.

I'm given two choices, both feel like hell:
I would either be drafted, or go to jail.

BOOT CAMP

OK, maggots!
Everywhere you go, you better run
Don't ever call your rifle a gun!
The first word out of your mouth better be, "Sir"
Or you'll be walking around in a blur.

It may kill me or you, but I'll make, you a man:
The best trained killers to ever hit Nam!
You will kill for the country and the corps
Your ass is mine, not mamma's anymore.

If you can't shoot the enemy, stab him with a knife.
One way or another, you will take his life:
Rip out his eyes, tear out his throat
Gut him, like you would a pig or a goat.

You will be trained killers, I want you to understand
Trained killers, each and every man.

OLD WARRIORS NEVER CRY

I never said what I had in my head.
War's glory was what John Wayne, and they, led
I follow in their wake by the tests I take,
I'm sworn in for my country's sake.

I want to make them proud, my uncle and dad,
I will give the war all I have
Why then do these warriors seem so sad?

After straining at the bit through thirty days of training
I'm a young Marine with my good-bye's remaining.
These two warriors take me to the bus
Time is fleeting, and history's not discussed.

The announcement says it's time to seat,
Our throats are dry and no one can speak.
Suddenly all I see is their wet cheeks.

I thought old warriors never cry....
Perhaps this was our last good-bye
Or even worse, maybe I would die.

Now, I realize, tears held back for years
Just gave birth to many fears.

GENERAL ORDERS

You better learn your General Orders
Learn them well.
If you don't know the answer
You'll think you died and went to hell.

TO TAKE CHARGE
TO WALK MY POST
TO REPORT ALL VIOLATIONS
TO REPORT ALL CALLS

You better have the answers
Or out of nowhere comes a kick to the balls.

TO QUIT MY POST
TO RECEIVE THE OKAY AND PASS IT ON
TO TALK TO NO ONE EXCEPT
TO GIVE THE ALARM

If you memorize all of these
You may escape a lot of harm.

TO CALL THE CORPORAL OF THE GUARD
TO SALUTE ALL OFFICERS
TO BE ESPECIALLY WATCHFUL AT NIGHT

May God be with you
If you don't get these right.

BAYONET

Spread your feet
Shoulder-width apart,
Put your left foot forward
Thrust for the heart,

Keep your hips level,
Keep your body facing front,
You better learn it well
If your going to be a grunt.

Running out of ammo
Is one hell of a thought
You better train well
In case you're put in this spot.

THE 45

M1911A1 automatic pistol caliber .45
This hand weapon kept a lot of men alive.

Approximate weight is three pounds
With a magazine capacity of seven rounds.

A semi-automatic that easily fires fast,
With a trigger you can squeeze
Standing, laying, or on your knees.

KILL, KILL, KILL

They made us into fighting machines
Accomplished this, while we were still teens;
Along with a uniform khaki green
We were given a name called Marines.

Kill, kill, kill,
We passed the test.
Kill, kill, kill,
There is no rest.
Kill, kill, kill,

Now, we're one of the best.

Rifle M-14

This rifle's called the M-14,
Fires a 7.62 caliber that is mean:
Air coiled, gas operated, magazine fed
Leaves many enemy wounded or dead.

A full magazine weighs over eleven pounds
And easily holds twenty lethal rounds---
Forty four inches long with a barrel of twenty two
Train with this rifle, until your aim is true.

It's minimum trigger pull is 5.5 pounds,
It goes to work putting out some rounds.
A maximum range of 460 meters, for a hit that's true
Hope it doesn't happen to be sighted in on you.....

LEARN WELL

"Fall in, fall out," I wish
They'd make up their mind.
"Fall in," time to march
And form a straight line.

"Parade rest, at ease,
And right face, too."
All this helps to make
A Marine out of you.

"Left face, about face,
Halt, now, double time."
This sure can mess
With your mind.

"Right flank, left flank,
Half step, back step, too.
Once you get it right,
We will let up on you."

"Order arms, trail arms,
Port arms, get it right!
Present arms, inspect arms,
It might take all night.

Sling arms, stack arms,
Open ranks, dismissed."
Even if we do it right
He still sounds pissed.

THE TITLE

It can't be explained
It's something special in the name
I fought hard and suffered to get
One thing I'd never regret

They said I wouldn't make it
Even kicked me around
Only now it's more important
To take the lumps, stand my ground

Once I received the title
Just as many had done before
I asked if it's worth dying for

Time came to put me to the test
My country called, I am the best

I carry the title with pride
And head for the plane
Sixty men in combat gear
Sharing the same name

Semper Fi----What does it mean?
"Always Faithful"
Once a marine, always a marine

THIRTY DAY LEAVE

Boot camp was over I was a lean mean little runt
MOS--0311 meant I was a grunt
Thirty day pass, then restricted to base---
I was soon headed for another place

It was good to see my three brothers, mom, and dad
I tried to have fun, but inside felt very bad.
I said good-bye, but couldn't say I was headed for war,
Mom had a way of knowing and cried at the door

Dad couldn't speak, we shook hands and he left the room
Then I hugged my brothers', had to be back by noon.
My older brother drove me back to San Diego, a long way.
First time we made the trip, and we didn't have much to say.

It would be a long time before I'd see him again,
He stuck out his hand and hugged me. I tried to hide the pain within,
There wasn't anything we could do and nothing more to say;
Marines aren't suppose to cry, but I lost the battle, as he drove away.

Take care, brother.

PART III

VIETNAM

TRAINED

We headed for the plane
Trained killers every man
Young men filled with hate
Headed for Vietnam.

Going to fight for Old Glory
The red, white, and blue
When we reach Nam
We'll do what we have to do.

There is little fear
They trained us well
No one resisted
This trip straight to hell.

THOUGHTS ABOUT NAM

On the plane headed for Nam, not knowing what to find,
I couldn't believe all the horrid thoughts that flooded my mind.
I wondered if I could kill a man when it came down to him or me,
I had a feeling it wouldn't be long and the answer I would see.

I wondered if my friend got hit
Would I have the guts to help him through the thick of it.
I wondered, too, what I'd do if I lost an arm, leg, or even an eye
Then suddenly it dawned on me, there's a possibility, I might die!

It was going to be a long trip so I tried to get some rest
My mind was racing and no one around to help get this off my chest.
There wasn't much talking on the plane and no one kidded around
It didn't take long to see the airstrip, we were about to touch down.

WELCOME TO NAM

We landed in the war zone, a hell hole called Da Nang,
That was our last encounter, we caught another plane.
We descended to Dong Ha, a fire base, close to the front---
MOS-0311, identified me as a grunt.

I reported to Mike Company, combat group 3/4
Next stop was the supply tent to prepare to enter war
I told the Sarge' behind the counter, I needed 782 gear
He looked, shook his head and said, "Your still wet behind the ears."

Sarge' said to me, "Your getting younger all the time
Clean your rifle good Marine, tomorrow you are the front line."
I found a tent full of holes and dropped my gear at the door,
With my M-14 across my knees, my hands worked on the bore.

Mike Company was in the bush, but got back real soon,
They went down to the wire and got in just past noon.
They looked old and ragged, but were young, proud, teens
Small in their company, these are combat Marines.

THIS STRANGE LAND VIETNAM

Vietnam is such a strange land:
A place inside the jungle
Where man hunts man.

Who is better or worse?
It matters little,
We all suffer the same curse.

There is no shame, only pain.
Some have been known
To go insane.

NEW HOME

Barbed wire fence
Three rolls high:
Do it right, Marine,
Or else you'll die!

Fill up sand bags
A shovel at a time:
Move up front, Marine,
Set another mine!

Set up trip flares,
Fix a killing zone---
Dig your hole deep, Marine,
Because this is your new home!

YOUR GEAR

Put on our helmets,
Flack jackets, canteens.
Saddle up, move out,
We are U.S. Marine's.

Get our C-Rations
Our rifles and ammo, too,
Everywhere we go
This goes with you.

Fill up our pockets,
Put in some night flares,
Snap on grenades,
Secure our K-bars.

Word has it
We are on a big push
So we slowly start
Into the bush.

NEW GUY

Three days old in Vietnam, the company was sent into the bush.
The mission was to stop the NVA from mounting another push.
I was told to walk point, that's where all new guys go--
I kept my eyes moving fast and stalked the jungle real slow.

The point man first in view is always the first to die.
He is positioned as a target until there is another new guy.
I searched the jungle, like deer hunting for my first buck.
No one befriended the new guy, as a rule, it was bad luck.

After tensely humping for hours in a jungle of massive green hell,
I met my first Viet Cong on a trail that was bent but traveled well.
The Viet Cong shouldered an AK-47 and I commanded a M-14.
He had his rifle on his back and mine, was chest level on a jungle sling.

I stood there a million seconds, we were transfixed eye to eye--
Cold sweat of terror tricked down my spine, I knew one of us must die.
I didn't want to kill him, but he made a move at last.
My bullets tore at his body before I heard the blast.

Guys then accepted me, and I was no longer the new guy in 'Nam.
I broke the bad luck spell by the killing of a man.

TWELVE MONTHS

I had a hole for a home
With a hard dirt bed.
Everything was too real,
It left scars in my head.

I crossed rivers
With water up to my chest,
Burned off leaches,
And had no time to rest.

I had bullets suddenly rake
My hiding place,
And watched the guy next to me
Lose his face.

When someone yelled,
"Fire in the hole!"
I laid there twitching,
With twelve months to go.

CLEAN RIFLE

Take apart the rifle,
Remove the bolt, pull out the spring.
Strip it down
And make it clean.

Pull out the piston
And strip it to the bone--
A clean rifle can make a difference,
If you want to make it home.

Make sure there is
No dirt or rust.
To survive,
This is a must.

HOW MUCH LONGER

"Hey, new guy,
How much longer will you be over here?"
They loved doing this,
I replied, "Two weeks and one year."

They would laugh a lot, clean their rifles,
And had jungle rot,
"Hey, new guy, before you leave,
Each village will have a telephone."

"Man, before you're out of here
You will be able to call home."
"Hey, new guy,
How much time to go, over here?"

I said, "One year, one week,
And a day."
"Man, by that time you'll be able
To drive home on a freeway."

I didn't like this game
And I didn't want to play,
But when you're the new guy
It's another small price to pay.

TO RULE

The king of the jungle isn't king anymore:
The lion's been replaced by the Marines in the Vietnam war.
Yes, I'm one of the kings, it's plain to see.
There's no one as wretched, vile, or sneaky as a grunt can be.

The crown is a steel helmet on my head,
My power is established by how many enemy I leave dead.
The throne is a bunker to rule my domain,
As long as I rule nothing that moves remains.

You wont see a rod or staff, just my M-14--
When passing judgment, all you'll feel is a burning hot sting.
I'm sent to rule twelve months, plus one.
All eyes fear the path of my gun.

I'm picked to be king, by our fellow man,
Sent to rule this place in Vietnam.
I'm given power to play God--
Rule this land over which we trod.

The Bible had lepers with ugly brown spots.
We had our unclean, their affliction was jungle rot.
In the Bible a river turned blood red.
Grunts do that, too, by leaving many enemy dead.

People think God's ways are cruel,
But you've got to be tough if your going to rule.

ENVISIONED WAR

The chopper's in fast position,
Ready to touch down.
It's wheels are ten feet
Off the ground.

The back side is lowered
And the front end is high--
We're dumped out the back
With no time to wonder why.

We tumbled to the ground
With man on top of man.
We fired and moved for cover,
We had to make a stand.

Another dropped a load,
Monster grasshoppers on my knee caps,
The orders say to hold out all night,
By morning be back to un-bait the traps.

We are expendable because
They can always bring in more.
Shock, abandon, and fear into telling the truth,
Isn't how I envisioned war.

FIRST PRAYER

I ran for a hole at the sound of artillery rounds whistling in,
Thinking the world, must be coming to an end.
I dove in a bunker and held my helmet tight
And began praying, wondering, if I even had the right.

God, I'm new at this, I've never prayed before,
Can you please help me get through this war.
Lord, I believe in you and want to let you know
Oh Lord, will you please bless this hole.

I'm just trying to stay alive from day to day.
I don't want to kill anyone, just keep the Cong away.
I want to do what's right, I don't want them dead
Lord, please keep them out of sight.

Speechless and yours, I really am your friend,
Thanks for listening, so be it ....
Amen.

THE HEAT

Fighting in the jungle, (the heat is unreal)
I keep moving, even though it's uphill.
I get a feeling, that I need to slow down,
I can feel the enemy, I know they are around.

The feeling gets stronger, (goes right to the bone)
The deeper we push into the unknown.
Bullets come thrashing out from the jungle green
It's time to get down, dirty, and mean.

Return fire is given so fast it's hard to explain,
For one brief moment everything is insane.
First I'm scarred then I'm raging mad
When it's over, I'm just thankful and glad.

I thought it was over, but it's not quiet yet
There are still two miles to go, before the sun sets.
We can't let the NVA know where we dig in,
Before the sun sets, this will happen again and again.

DIG IN

Use an E-tool
To dig yourself a hole:
If you get hit, then reaching it,
Will be your main goal.

Forget blisters,
Just slam the tip into the dirt,
Your hands will go numb,
Way beyond hurt.

You may dig for hours,
Just to get half-way
Then you're told, "saddle up,"
Decided not to stay.

BOUNCING BETTY

The sunlight happened to hit just right and I saw a tiny flash ahead:
It was a trip wire that could have left me dead.
I followed that wire, wondering where it would lead
A bush attached with a bouncing Betty, could have made me bleed.

Bouncing Betty had a trigger that bounced a small grenade knee-high,
Designed to blow off legs to the crotch, chances are you wouldn't die,
It's intended to wound so you'd suffer a lot, and slow you down,
Take you permanently out of action, so you'd no longer be around.

The squad leader said "Disarm it," a task I didn't like.
I noticed another wire under the bush, just to my right.
As I uncovered the wire, everyone started moving back
I carefully followed it and uncovered a second trap.

I used a twig to move the leaves and could clearly see the nose:
A large artillery round with a double trap exposed.
I heard a whisper, it was the squad leader, he motioned to come in,
And asked, "Do you think you can undo this trap?" Chances were very slim.

We can't just leave it as it is, another unit could pass by,
If they didn't notice it, then men could die.
Then Gooding came to me with a grenade in his hand
"Lets toss one of these on each trap, what's a few more holes in this land"

We'd expose our position, the NVA would know where we were at
But we all agreed to take the chance, it was just too big a trap.
Gooding looked at me after the squad moved out, and I looked back at him
Then, I said "let's haul ass, my friend," as we pulled our pins.

The grenades landed next to the targets as we bolted out of there,
We knew just when to hit the dirt, heard the blasting sound fill the air.
Those two booby traps, turned out to be five,
If we'd stumbled into this one there would hardly been a man left alive....

Just another hour, out of another day, out of three hundred sixty five.

DEADLY PREMONITION

Sunset Byrd came to my bunker, looking long past sad
I told him I'd lend my ears, to any problems he might have.
He took off his helmet and slowly sat down
Then placed his face into his hands and stared at the ground.

I told him I would help, but he'd have to let me in,
"Just tell me what it is, you know I am your friend."
At last he looked up, and then, he began to cry,
Shook his head in agony and said, "Man, I'm going to die!"

I didn't know how to answer, he took me by surprise.
My hands were tied as I sat and watched the tears flow from his eyes.
I said I'd give him full support, and wouldn't let him get out of my sight,
But he smiled, "We can't change fate," then he said, "Good-night"

We loaded into the helicopters at daylight, then we were off into the air,
We sat in silence, knowing that death was down there.
The chopper quickly dropped us off and we formed a staggered line,
Byrd was told to take point, and the flank was mine.

Cautiously we moved uphill, the VC booby trapped it well.
Flying bullets triggered the land mines and blew the ridge to living hell!
We suffered heavy casualties, the VC hardly seen,
I lost my friend, he was a mighty fine Marine.

I couldn't watch out for him on this day, nor could he, for me
I wonder if it's true about fate: was this really meant to be?

MY FRIEND

Left the chopper on the hill top, a long way from base,
Then started hacking our way through the hip high grass.
We approached a savage battle without even a prayer
We were pinned in positions while bullets controlled the air.

We couldn't move forward and we couldn't move back,
We listened to screams while the blue sky turned black.
My friend Gooding laid a base of fire while we were behind the hill
He emptied his machine gun, his nick name was Wild Bill.

The hill was VC booby trapped, my arm turned bloody red,
Several of my friends were wounded, and one friend ahead lay dead.
Eight will never fight again,
Among them my brother, most vital friend.

My friends were now dead or wounded, and Gooding was headed home.
Time to reload my rifle, as I stood there alone
The choppers moved skyward, and I watched till they're almost out of sight,
I said "Take care brothers, you fought one hell of a fight!"

MY BUNKER

I finish my bunker, have to dig in hard ground,
With sand bag walls, humid heat, and excitement abound
I look at my fortress with pride
Then the fun begins, I get to furnish the inside!

I crawl through the opening the size of a doggie door,
I enjoy decorating the inside, it helped to forget the war.
I think I'd hang a chandelier in the middle of the wall
With my K-Bar I carve away dirt and rock and watch it fall,

I carve an indentation 4" X 4" deep and 8" high
Just enough room for a chandelier, (I learned this from another guy)
I took out my candle, a cherished possession.
Having a candle, for me, this was an obsession.

I place it in the slot and with my lighter touch the wick
I am one hell of a carpenter and pick the perfect spot.
I place my chair in the corner and cut away the wall
Decorating my bunker was really a ball!

I leave a two foot mound of dirt on the floor,
Few people know of these luxuries, while I am fighting in this war.
My chandelier begins to melt while I watched it flicker and glow
I kick back and re-read my letters in my apartment, my bunker, my hole.

YOUR SON, MY FRIEND

Living in a hole
With one candle inside
Writing to his folks
So they'd know how he died.

FRIEND

The paper is blank
I can't find words to say
That your son
Was blown away.

A FRIEND

I don't know why he died
Or why we are here.
Oh damn! the letter is spotted
With another tear.

MY FRIEND

This is a sick place
Writing parents is my "free time" task.
I wonder if writing this letter
Will this for me be asked.

YOUR SON

SWAMP WATER

I bent down to the swamp and
Filled up my canteen,
It was infested
But no longer meant a thing,

I need to have water,
So I drink the brine,
Just brush away the bugs and
Try to avoid the slime,

I dropped two tablets in the canteen,
Shook the liquid well,
It takes thirty minutes---
Sometimes the wait is pure hell

But wait you will,
It only matters that it's wet,
The dead insects floating
Just try to forget.

BLACK TAPED EDGE

Two steel magazines
One facing up
The other facing down,

Bind them together,
Slowly wrap black tape
Around and around....

This is the thing to do.
Now push twenty rounds in each,
This will give the edge to you.

CAM LO

We are choppered into the jungle
Not knowing where to go,
We hump the bush, reach the objective
Get out our E-tools, and dig a hole.

We set up a machine gun and
Fix a killing zone,
Then word comes down the line that
For a week or two, this will be our home.

At dawn barbed wire is choppered in,
We string it all over the place
And ask, "why we are doing this?"
To make a fire base.

What are they going to call this place,
We really want to know.
This fire base
Will be called Cam Lo.

We work for weeks with that barbed wire,
Fighting, and digging holes in between.
Our hands are all torn up
And the heat is really mean.

Once the base is secure
We're choppered in good supplies,
Then tanks and trucks roll in,
There are quite a lot of guys.

These guys take over the lines and bunkers and
Thank us for the work we'd done,
Then we start building outhouses and mess tent,
It's starting to look like fun.

We are told that tomorrow
A hot meal and even a shower, was on the way,
But then we're told to saddle up
The NVA were spotted and we must head out today.

HEAR WHAT I SEE

Screaming, screaming, screaming,
Yelling out in pain,
"Corpsman! corpsman! corpsman!"
Could drive a man insane

I hear low pitched moans
And high pitched screams
I run to help all the wounded,
Dying Marines.

"Help me, I'm hit over here!"
I hear a voice in my head,
I run to his side and hold him up,
But he's not wounded, he's dead.

Then there are voices that like to come
In the middle of the night:
They call out until I awake screaming,
"Hold on man, you'll be all right"

I feel their pain
And I feel their need.
When all is quiet, I see the wounds
And can hear them bleed.

Now, I've heard enough
And I just don't want to hear anymore,
But I can't turn off the front line,
I'm surrounded by sounds of war.

THE NEXT ROUND

That round was close,
I heard the steel fly over my hole
Where the next one hits,
I will never know.

The noise is horrifying,
And I hate to just sit and wait...
I try to control my fear,
Since the next round might bring my fate.

The earth shakes a little
And the dirt falls in,
The rounds are falling closer,
I hope it soon will end.

The next round hits hard
And fills the hole with dust--
This is as bad as it gets
And praying is a must.

The next round will tell a story,
It will let me know
If I will be left alive,
Or if it will be my time to go.

Then I hear another round fired,
It comes whistling in--
I'm really talking to God,
Hope he's listening, Amen!

Another round hits, my helmet falls off,
And I feel very odd.
It brings a blur to my eyes,
But I'm still alive and I thank God.

NO MORE NICE GUY

I was such a nice guy
When I was sent to Nam
I may be no Boy Scout,
But was as good as the next man.

I had no desire
To hurt anyone,
I'd just do my time,
And then go home.

I thought I would never
Have to kill
But that was before my friend died,
They shot Wild Bill.

Pay they did,
One through eight
No more nice guy,
I became crazed with hate.

I could make a man die slow,
Or kill him fast.
A snapped mind wants vengeance,
It's payment for the past,

What a way to learn
To make suffering last.

DOOR GUNNER

He didn't stand out much in the Vietnam war,
But he was one guy the NVA tried for.
He stood inside the chopper door with eyes like a hawk
He didn't say much, since he wasn't there to talk.

When choppers came in, he went to work,
His bullets ripped up the jungle, forcing the enemy to dirt.
He'd swing his machine gun, side to side--
Not many would challenge him, those who did, died.

We loaded wounded under his cover,
He was mean and lean, like a big brother.
There were empty brass casings all over the floor,
Smoke and fire came out the chopper door.

The blades whirled overhead
While we loaded our wounded and our dead.
As we got the chopper ready for flight
The door gunner blazed on, and continued the fight.

All the extra weight made the chopper move real slow,
But once it was up and turning, it was ready to go.
There were empty brass casings that rained down from the blue,
It was big brother, the door gunner, still watching over you.

REVENGE

I'm sending out a 7.62,
It's target is a VC.
I hope my aim is true.

I'd Like to kill a Cong today.
The death of my friends
Makes me feel this way.

I need revenge, but will make it clean.
It's more than he would do,
My enemy is mean.

He wants to die for his country,
I won't make him scream or shout.
I'll do my damnedest
To help him out.

A LITTLE REST

Now I lay me down to rest
M-14 across my chest,
All I want is to get some sleep
But my tense muscles are ready to leap.

One eye's open, the other's shut tight
I can tell already, it's gonna be a long night.
I hear a grave rat's squeaky sound
Searching for food and clawing the ground,

Someone yells, "Incoming!" there's nowhere to go
The rat nestles me for safety, none can leave this hole.
It feels good to finally get some rest
I stand up and knock the grave rat from my chest.

ONE ROUND

One bullet fired, just one round--
Like pulling a carpet, we all went down.
I Lay there sweating, awaiting the next shot,
Knowing a sniper has me on the spot.

My eyes strain at the bushes, I gaze into the trees
Fear keeps me, below my knees
Is he still out there, did he run away
I won't stick my head up, it's to high a price to pay

As a rule, fire only one shot, so not to give my position away
(They were smart, these NVA).
Word comes to move out, and I must stand
Sure hope his cross hairs aren't on this man.

First I'm squatting, then kneeling, now I stand,
I survived another shot fired in Vietnam.

HIDE AND SEEK NAM STYLE

The sun goes down and the day fades away,
Word comes down, the second squad's going out to play.
Like hide and seek played as a kid for fun
In this game losers die playing tag with a gun.

Sneak out at night with your face covered in black,
Hope you hide first and pray you make it back,
Reach you ambush sight and carefully dig in,
Hope the sun comes up and this game won't begin.

Soon the other players are heard, just up the trail,
Everyone opens up, it's the game rule.
Fight fierce to send Cong to hell, and hope it won't last long--
Worst fears are realized when everything goes wrong.

VC throws grenades while screaming fills the air,
Two friends are killed, but there's no time to care.
The battle rages on until we see the rays from a rising sun,
The body count shows that our side has won.

Nam style hide and seek, a game which never ends
The worst part about it is no one ever wins.

DEATH AWAITS

I see a trip wire and pass it down the line,
It's Indian country and the point man found a mine.
We start moving, but we go slow,
I see a pungi pit, then a spider hole.

We walk past bunkers, dug by the NVA,
Hoping no one is home, just hoping they are all away,
We clear the bunkers without hearing a sound,
My stomach is in knots and I slowly look around.

Now we go down the ridge, feeling chilled to the bone,
And run into the NVA on their way home.
I'm going to puke, the bullets are coming my way.
Oh, not again, not again, today.

I throw up on the ground,
Then fire ten more rounds.
The bullets rip through the trees.
They fire back, so I get on my knees,

Change magazines and stand my ground.
I'm strong and steady and look all around.
Then word comes for us to move out real slow,
Death awaits us this we know.

GRAVE RATS

I live in a bunker,
But this place is not my own.
If careless bits of food are on my face or lips,
Soon I'm not alone.

At dusk the grave rats come out
And I announce they're here to forage,
With, "Get this mother off me!"
It's my first hand knowledge.

None of them are small.
They are large, hairy, football size.
They look bigger when they bite, and wake me up,
Staring with their two red eyes.

Imagine their confusion
When this grave man isn't dead.
It is an inescapable fact of bunker living,
Another night time dread.

Grave rats adjust to the status of their meals quickly,
These beasts don't mind,
But I found ways to keep from becoming
Their night delight, in very little time.

COFFEE NAM STYLE

I empty my bread can,
Then find the heat tab, coffee, and cream.
Next I hold the can
And punch some holes around the seam.

I heat and eat from this can,
And must hurry to get through,
Having enough heat left to boil coffee
Is an art few can do.

I take water from my canteen
And fill up the empty can,
Then set it on the heat tab,
This is how I make coffee in Nam.

Once the water is boiling,
I dump in the coffee, sugar, and cream.
It's time to relax and enjoy.
Out of a can of nothing, I made a grunt's real dream.

THE PONCHO

The poncho
Is a pull-over rain coat
That can be used as a sled.

This poncho
Can also be used as a blanket
But more often used
To drag the wounded and dead.

MY PONCHO

TRADE OUT THE M-14

We were brought in from the bush
And didn't know a thing,
Then issued new rifles
Called the M-16.

The M-14 was a solid rifle
It worked, and served me well--
I didn't want an M-16,
Like a plastic rifle made by Mattel.

It didn't help us much
Because this rifle frequently jammed.
Grunts needed rifles that worked
While walking the bush in Nam.

Often lives were lost
Because this rifle would choke,
They expected us to fight
With a rifle that was a joke.

So many fears and other things
To contend with in Nam.
At times I could only pray
That this rifle wouldn't jam.

CLAYMORE

It's called a claymore mine
With over 100 steel pellets inside.
When it was set off,
It would cut out a path very wide.

We'd stick it in the ground
And run a wire back to our hole,
That way all its destruction
Would be in our control.

It had a back-flash
That could take off your head.
If you weren't down in a hole
You could easily end up dead.

There were other reminders
That would really help to you get down,
Like times the enemy would sneak in at night
And turn the claymore around.

LIE AND WAIT

All is quiet, not a rustle, not even a sound.
I'm lying in an ambush site with darkness all around.
Then comes a shot of gunfire and all I can hear
Is unearthly screams, born from fear.

The radioman is dead and the squad leader, too.
Word comes down, "Adams, tell us what to do."
I crawl over dead NVA and move into the killing zone
"Fall back, form a 360, lets get the dead and wounded home!"

Side by side the rest of us form a circle on the ground
And check our rifles quietly, then slip in another round.
Each man is silent, hoping enough of the NVA fell dead
There will be no more fighting (though none of this is said).

We lie and wait with no more to be done.
We just lie and wait, for the rising sun.

THE CORPSMAN

The Corpsman had nerves of steel:
He ran to the wounded all over that hill.
He must have figured he couldn't be hit
Because he kept running, even through the thick of it.

I thought he had to be insane:
He always responded when he heard his name.
He carried his bag, close at his side.
If it wasn't for him, more men would have died.

The Corpsman is a man among men:
Willing to risk his life again and again.
We couldn't honor this man enough.
He was special, and he was tough.

The Corpsman saved lives (even mine a time or two):
Through raging bullets, he would head for you.
He was someone to talk with and he'd always be your friend.
He really is a man among men.

DUST OFF

I tossed a smoke grenade
To let the choppers know
The wounded and dead at LZ
Were ready to go.

I reached up wanting to snatch
The Medivac from the air
With good reason,
My wounded brothers were there.

He had flash-burns in his eyes and
A gash on his head, so I took my hand
And desperately reached out
To make the chopper land.

I would die for my brothers
If that be the cost...
Standing tall made me easy target
Until my brothers were dusted off.

NO RICH KIDS

Did you ever see a rich kid
fight in Nam
With jungle rot
And a rifle in his hand?

Think about it ,
Think real hard,
Is there a Rolls or Jag
Parked in your front yard?

I met mostly poor guys,
Many were black--
I never saw a rich kid
Digging C-rats from his pack.

It's okay to send poor kids,
There were plenty to be found,
I never met a kid
From the better side of town.

In Nam, I had no trouble rapping,
I understood the talk,
Fighting and dying was done
By kids from the block.

Let this be a lesson
Before the next war rolls around,
Fighting and dying was done
By kids from the poor side of town.

IF IT MOVES

A Gook is sitting around
Eating someone's dog
While I'm eating C-rations
Sitting on a log.

I can see his solid black teeth
From eating beetle nuts.
Word comes down
To zippo the huts.

The Gook's now running,
All our meals are forgotten,
Just another day full
Of everything rotten.

I hate the order
But have no say,
Just do what I'm told
If it moves, blow it away.

NEW NAME

The rich are in the rear area, the fighting's done by poor men
Off to my left, I hear a scream, someone needs a corpsman.
A Marine has been hit and he is crying,
All over that mountain are sounds of men dying.

Bullets force me behind a log with nowhere else to go,
I look around the end and bring my rifle up real slow,
There is no choice, there's incoming here, Jack's ordered to go fight
With still no urge to kill, I found him in my sight.

The enemy is moving now and I wish he would run
Away from me, because he is a target for my gun.
It kicks a slam into my shoulder--
In that instant, that VC's life is over.

I had to kill him, it was meant to be.
It came down to him or me,
I took his life, I'm the taker
Now guys call me the Widow Maker.

MIND RAPE

No laughing or crying
Only pain and dying
A whole boy comes to Vietnam
Will leave a broken man.

Hey, Marine, what the hell have you got?
Those oozing scabs is something called jungle rot.
Living in holes day and night and all alone,
Knowing that next bullet could send you home.

Breakfast, lunch, and dinner from a can
What a mind rape, this war's called Vietnam.

QUESTIONS, WHAT ANSWERS

Look at the bright fog
Rolling in; over there
A toxin, Agent Orange,
Is changing the air.

What is it used for,
What does it mean?
Thinning the jungle
For you, Marine.

Buy from the lowest bidder,
Poisons are no exception,
Dump it all over Nam
It's our fatal last deception.

I can't believe that,
Do you mean things can get worse?
Yes, raining Agent Orange
Will take you home with a lethal curse.

THE MARINES ARE COMING

All the villagers ran away,
They were told that the Marines
Were on their way.

We were there to help,
But that's not what they were being told.
The NVA told the villagers stories
That would turn your blood ice cold.

In order to become a Marine
You must kill your parents, back in the USA.
This was the first test to become a Marine,
The price you had to pay.

They told the villagers that Marine's
Must kill three kids and eat one while running.
Shit, I would have left that village, too,
If I heard the Marines were coming!

LETTER TO A WARRIOR

Howdy Bro,

I had to get this off my chest,
Until I finish this letter, I won't rest.
Thank you for saving my life...
Your family is proud, especially your son and wife.

Even here, we found a laugh or two--
Man, I'm going to miss you!
Six more months until I'm headed home.
I miss you Bro, I feel so alone.

Remember Cam Lo?
Eighty eight rounds hit next to our hole.
We'd fight over C-rat's, to see who would eat lima beans,
Just more life and times of the United States Marines.

Well bro, I have nothing more to say.
Just wanted you to know I'm sorry you got killed yesterday.
I'm going to burn this now, so it will send smoke and ash into the air,
Be sure to grab it, because I know you are up there.

Please spread my name and tell them I'm a nice guy,
For tomorrow it may be my turn to die.

Your friend

VIETNAM AND COUNTING

REFLEX

The bullets found the target
That was coming into view,
I shot him dead.
Now, another young life is through.

NO PAIN

It was a clean shot,
He felt no pain,
I killed him quick
And didn't know his name.

DEAD

He was not the first,
He was number four.
I want to lose count
But can't, I tried before.

AND COUNTING

READY YOURSELF

Burn a log till it turns black,
Rub soot on your hands and face,
Get ready Jack.

Tape your dog tags and say a prayer,
For in ten minutes
You could be dead out there.

The night is theirs, that's what they say,
But tonight is ours,
If they chance this way.

THE LATRINE SCENE

Come with me for some front line fun,
And learn the art of burning human dung.
Under the outhouse is half a fifty gallon drum
Brimming with human waste. Just watch how it's done.

It takes three to drag it out and set it level on the ground,
Then pour in five gallons of diesel and stir it all around.
A splash of gas will help to keep it burnin'.
The black smoke it gives off is an acrid smell of dung and urine.

This job puts a body to the test--
After fifteen minutes of stirring, your arms will need a rest.
When the flames go out, just pour on more diesel and gas,
It takes the same amount of time whether you're stirring slow or fast.

Keep moving until there's only black ash left in the can,
Then dig another hole, that's how it's done in Vietnam.
Drop all the ashes into the hole.
Thank God, only two more to go.

TUNNEL RAT

"Adams, up front!"
Those words sent fear into the heart of this grunt,
In a country full of hills, unsure where we were at.
When summoned up front, I knew I'd be a tunnel rat.

Just this side of the DMZ
The captain pointed at the hole and gave a .45 to me.
I stripped off my gear and dropped into the hole.
I kept moving, but went real slow.

I lit a zippo and saw a rotting body lying ahead.
God only knows how long he'd been dead.
The smell was ungodly, the stench extremely bad.
I moved forward fast, but it took all I had.

When I had to do this I'd break into a cold sweat.
I hardly speak of those times, but I will never forget.
I'd light my lighter again once the tunnel became a large space,
And find bags of rice, guns and ammo, all over the place.

I'd break through a bamboo roof, then all could see.
They'd pull out the rice, guns, and ammo, and then me.

CHRISTMAS IN VIETNAM

On December 25th, spending Christmas in Vietnam
Was a day that brought sadness to every man.
We were pulled out of the bush and told to stand in line--
It wasn't enough to make us have a good time.

A gift laden truck rolled in, to us Marines.
A stampede to those boxes indeed changed the scene.
Mine was heavy, I felt like a child,
I waited for my friends with curiosity that was wild.

I found a quiet spot to sit real quick, and tore the string and all.
Out tumbled dog food cans with a note, "Eat hardy, fucking animal."
It was the Christmas spirit sent from USA,
And it was confusing to be thought of this way.

My friends approached with three records and a razor.
We were ridiculed by pranks, just more sufferings of war.
Let me tell how well another brother fared:
Three used rubbers and a note, "Your girl was nice, glad you are there"

I offered to share my dog food, then insults changed the mood.
Santa and the reindeer seemed funny and we became pretty lewd.
The closeness we shared helped take away feeling homesick
We were brothers and Marines, spending Christmas in Vietnam, 1966.

B-52 FLY-BY

Pass it on, it's called the B-52,
For the enemy it was bad news.
We'd get into a bunker just to play it safe
The B-52 would drop close and circle the base.

We could hear the bombs explode
When they dropped their load,
Then a smoky wall encircled us, real slow.
How many bombs were dropped, we didn't know.

The B-52 would hit it's mark, even if it was tight,
Then we'd watch it fly high until it went out of sight.
We'd scream and clap and yell our praise.
Sorry Charlie, it was just one of those days.

The squad leader'd come by the bunker to give us the news
To move out at dawn and check damage done by the B-52.
It was an awesome sight to watch a bomber fly away.
We liked the B-52, it always made our day.

NAPALM

It didn't look like much,
Just a thin canister falling from the air.
You'd never believe the destruction
It would leave down there.

It would turn the jungle
A burned-out black,
Leaving the area so nothing
Could grow back.

Napalm never just fell,
It would tumble and glide.
After seeing the damage,
Be glad it was used by our side.

VIETNAM SHAKES

Everywhere you look,
There are wounded and dead,
Bullets striking all around,
Some just inches from your head.

PRAY

You are shaking so hard,
You feel like an ass.
It's not the first time,
And you know it will pass.

OVERCOME

Once your trembling stops,
You can chance a better view.
The Cong switched their firing,
For now, they've forgotten you.

COMPOSED

Snap off a grenade
And quickly pull the pin,
Toss it close the bunker,
Just not quite in.

SATISFIED

An explosion joins the den,
While smoke fills the air--
Up into the crater,
You put twenty rounds in there.

BEATING CHARLIE

I snapped in a magazine, slammed the bolt home.
It was time for revenge, I was feeling mean to the bone.
I made it through 10 months, now I'm no longer the same,
I'm good at beating Charlie at his own game.

I set out trip wires tied to a grenade--
He's walked into a few traps that I made.
I take a grenade, and pull the pin,
I had a can to put it in.

Then carefully I set it down.
He never failed to pick it up, now Charlie's no longer around.
Ten months of being under strain,
A way to release pressure is to beat Charlie at his own game.

MONSOON RAIN

Sitting in a hole
With the rain pouring down,
I couldn't see the Cong.
I wondered if they were around.

It was now the ninth rainy day,
So I pulled my poncho tight--
I smelled so bad,
It made it hard to sleep at night.

My poncho was a cover,
To help get my cigarette lit,
And sometimes a shelter,
When I had to take a shit,

I smoked, ate and slept in it,
Night and day.
Thank God, after taking a shit,
At least I could walk away.

LETTER HOME TO DAD

Dear Dad,

Just a short note to let you know that I'm still here.
Each day makes it closer to that month and one year.
I lost many friends and feel very heavy inside,
Everyone here feels that loss, but none have cried.

War is hell, worse than I thought it would be.
Now, I know why you never talked about your war with me.
Be proud of me for what I must do,
Your trust will see me through.

I made a mistake, saw grafts, kickbacks, such crime--
It's too late to change any of that, and I know I must finish my time.
I'd love to share my war with you, but know I must suffer it alone
Could we share a few beers, since I'll be old enough when I get home?

Your son,

DEAR JOHN

Honey,

Sorry I haven't written in such a long time.
(That's okay woman he's been fighting on the front line.)

Hope my letter finds you doing well.
(That's okay this is just a short visit to hell.)

Hope you'll understand, I fell for this guy Sam.
(She found a real man while he was fighting in Nam.)

Take care honey, I did love you dear.
(I should write and make it clear--
John was killed yesterday, he's no longer here.)

P.S. Dear John, shall I keep the ring?
(Bitch lost it all-- she lost a Marine!)

INCOMING

When I hear incoming, my blood runs icy cold--
It only takes once to learn this lesson,
After that, don't have to be told.

I run for a hole and pray
Hoping God will hear me and
Help me through this day.

The first round hits and the earth shakes!
Please Lord, don't let the next round
Bring my fate.

Rounds are falling and there's nothing I can do,
My mind wants to panic,
I fight to keep it cool.

They dropped twenty rounds, or maybe twenty-five--
It's silent! the attack is over and
I am still alive!

I thank the almighty with another prayer,
Head back to my hooch,
But it's no longer there.

I realize my only chance in prayer lay,
Since this insane activity
Happens about four times a day.

BAD NEWS

"Hey, Jack, check out this newspaper
The new guy just brought it in.
Check out the article about the Nam Vet,
Read what happened to him:"

Vietnam Vet returns home
Gets off the plane, all alone
Protesters hit him
He slaps one on the head
Protesters pull their guns
Shoots the Nam Vet dead

"Can you believe this story,
Believe that it's true?
Guess I would believe anything
After all we've been through.

What are we going to do,
Don't want to stay here and we can't go home.
I guess if we ever get out of here
Each man will be on his own.

I'm kind of lost for words brother,
I don't know what to say--
If we get out of Nam alive
We'll have to sweat surviving back in the USA.

MISTAKES

You are set up in an ambush site and it's half past two.
The quiet is broken by friendly fire,
It's your own guns pounding the hell out of you.

Jungle clothes are bloody red.
The new guy next to me
Now has no head.

Flipping, flopping, rolling around
I leap on the body and pin him down:
The noise might bring in another round.

It was his first day, by a mistake, he is dead.
I'm sick and sorry, as someone takes his body
I reach down and pick up his head.

BAMBOO POLES

I found NVA bodies hanging from bamboo poles,
Lots of corpses in freshly dug holes.
The NVA drug off their own dead--
A way to mess with our heads.

They tied the bodies' hands and feet to a pole,
Then pick them up and away they'd go.
After a savage battle there's wounded and dead,
But not finding any enemy is an eerie dread.

It didn't take long to figure out what they did,
The body count went up after finding the ones they hid.

EYES

Look over these dead bodies,
It's OK,
These are my enemy,
The NVA.

They tried to overrun us,
It was their mistake,
There was no choice
But to seal their fate.

Bodies laying in the heat,
Twice the normal size,
No forgetting
The look in their eyes!

Look
In their eyes,
Their eyes,
Eyes...

M-79
(BLOOPER)

It was called the blooper
Because of the sound it made,
The M-79 fired
A small grenade.

It broke open like a shot gun,
Fired one round at a time,
Don't want to be in his sights,
This man with the M-79.

He fired it upward
Into the sky of blue,
He had to be good at judging distance
With his aim true.

We fought between a tree line,
Close enough to throw rocks at the NVA,
Then came the "bloop, bloop," sound
Of enemy getting blown away.

There's no hiding
From the M-79.
Our man walked them
Down the tree line,

The NVA decided
It was time to go.
Sometimes the grenadier
Was a one man show.

NO SCREAMING IN THE DARK

NO NOISE
Bullets went in and blood pumped out.
I wanted to scream and needed to shout.

PAIN
I didn't make a sound in the ambush sight.
There is Cong all over in the middle of the night.

MORE PAIN
I rocked back and forth, not making a sound.
Any noise would bring in another round.

A LOT MORE PAIN
I hear voices whisper that we must fall back.
I shouldered my rifle and picked up my pack.

TOO MUCH PAIN
Dawn is breaking and choppers are on the way.
Just a little longer, then, I can scream all day.
SCREAMING PAIN

THE VISIT

He came to visit in my hole,
Said there was some things that I should know.
Holding a list of men that had to go,
He smiled at me and moved real slow.

He was dressed in black with a hood over his head,
He said his job was collecting all the dead,
I asked if I had a chance to make it home,
He told me if I did, I'd be all alone.

I asked, "Who put you in charge and why a dead list keeper?"
He pulled the sickle from beneath his cape and said,
"Because I am the Grim Reaper."
I said, "Come on man, give me a break!
Put that back beneath your cape."

He said, "No way," there's a place on the handle
He wanted to put my notch;
That was when Donavan kicked my leg to wake me up
And said it was my turn to stand watch.

GOD IS NOT WITH THE MEN IN VIETNAM

Being told that God is not with the men in Vietnam
Is the worst kind of news for me and every man.
Lord, I really need to know You're walking point up ahead.
I need that extra guarantee, I don't want to wind up dead.

Let your light show me through the jungle, it's so dark and thick.
All this killing for no reason is enough to make me sick.
Could you move closer, Lord, and tell me why we're in this war?
No one here seems to know what we are killing for.

Thoult Shalt Not Kill is a commandment that You said
Since it's Your commandment, what about the men I've left dead?
I think about their mothers, fathers, sisters, and brothers, too.
My mind needs relief, the kind that can only come from You.

Is there more than one God, I really need to know.
I'm praying from my bunker while the VC's praying from his hole.
It seems crazy, knowing we are both asking God for the same thing
Let me be the one to make it through, let my enemy feel the sting.

Could you give the leaders some insight, let them come here and stay.
So many sons are dying, we lost twelve more today.
You lost a Son for a cause; but this is worthless, it can't be won.
You are the one with the power, can You get this deed done?

Let the leaders send their children, let their sons be the first to go.
They always send others, they don't want their sons to be full of holes.
They like to keep their kids safe, sitting back somewhere in school,
While the poor man's sons are dying, and the rich men continue to rule.

I still don't hear an answer, but I know You are doing Your best.
It is our leaders, not You, Lord, that got us into this mess.
Thanks for listening, please don't leave me, I need You to hang around,
I hear incoming and know You're okay, but I'm the target on the ground.

Until You answer, I'll keep doing what I was sent here to do.
When the time comes I will answer, Lord, straight to You.

LETTER HOME TO MOM

Dear Mom,

Just a short letter let you know that everything here is fine.
(I can't let her know that I'm right on the front line.)

I just sit around wondering which card game to play.
(I can't tell her that I killed two Viet Cong today.)

You will be glad to know that they keep us well fed.
(Why tell her the extra C-rats came from a guy who is dead.)

You may hear there's fighting, but honestly, that's way up the line.
(I can't tell her my best friend just stepped on a mine.)

Good news mom, I'll be home in late June.
(I can't tell her how six guys got killed by a rocket, at noon.)

Mom, don't you be worrying none, because I'm doing just fine.
(Why tell her about the killing, dying, and how I'm losing my mind.)

Sorry, Mom, it took so long for me to write.
(I can't tell her that for ten days, I've been in a savage fight.)

Take good care mom, and say, "Hi," to everyone.
(I'll just keep my mouth shut, until my time is done.)

As always,

Your Son

JUNGLE ROT

It starts with a break in the skin,
Soon it rots and then becomes a scab.
There are so many of us covered with them
And we wonder what we have.

The scabs just get bigger
And build into sores,
Then they burn and turn red.
Sure hope I don't get anymore.

Life in Vietnam
Is already bad enough.
Living in a hole with grave rats
And now this oozing pus.

I boil swamp water
And act as if its part of life's meal,
Then pour the liquid into the mini-craters,
And hope to God they heal.

The smell is unbelievable!
There's jungle rot on ole' Browns cheek,
It has completely eaten through and
He has it from his head to his feet.

I told him he has to leave when it's time to eat.
I tolerate it for a month or two, or maybe four,
This is life in the combat zone along the DMZ,
Jungle rot---misery--- just one more.

SHORT TIMER

"Hey, short timer, how much longer you got
Before your headed back to the world
And that permanent vacation spot?"

"Man, I'm so short, I can't talk to you
I may not even get to finish
Before this conversation is through."

"Hey, short timer, how short are you
Before your headed for the world
And a nice break that's long overdue?"

"Man, I'm so short, even standing on my tip toes
I could walk under the belly of a snake
And not even come close."

"Hey, short timer, tell me just how long
Till you get out of the land of the gooks
And the Viet Cong?"

"Man, I'm so short, my helmet covers me
Clear down to my boots
It's even hard for me to believe."

"Hey, short timer, I love your chuck and jive.
We might get hit tonight, so stay away from my hole
Everyone knows that no one leaves Nam alive."

SEARCH THEN DESTROY

I searched the villages
Looking for Cong.
And hoped to hell that
Nothing would go wrong.

They knew we were coming,
They'd been told by persons unknown.
The villages stood eerily empty,
As if they'd been picked to the bone.

Our orders said to burn
Everything to the ground.
With all the fire and smoke,
Nothing standing could be found.

The villagers didn't want our help,
They wanted us to die.
The place they once called home
Was now black ash in the sky.

KIDS ARE KIDS

We came from the south side one warm and sunny day,
The only ones who moved around, were scared kids running away.
I could smell the twigs burning that were keeping their meals hot,
And I saw their rice bowls sitting next to a big black pot.

I smiled to let them know that everything was okay.
It was a routine search of a village, that happened on our way.
Kids are kids, even in Nam.
It didn't take long for a girl to come to me and hold out her hand.

I patted my fatigues and found that I had
A C-ration of grape jelly for her, then she ran away glad.
I searched the huts and they seemed to be okay,
Then suddenly, bullets came flying my way.

They had been hiding the Viet Cong,
And a deadly battle started but didn't last long.
People began falling left and right--
The villagers were caught in the middle of this fight.

The enemy wasn't accountable for what they did,
The villagers were gunned down by the enemy they hid.
The VC ran into the jungle and for the village it was a sad day--
Couldn't believe the bodies of villagers expendable to the NVA.

A kid in the middle of a battle is just not a good place.
I stepped over her dead body and saw grape jelly on her face.
I looked into her lifeless brown eyes staring back at me,
War is no place for any kid to be.

NO SLACK AT ALL

"Just a few more stitches, Marine,
And a couple more days in the rack.
But don't start liking it,
Because soon you'll be going back."

"Just a few more stitches, Marine,
No sweat, it missed the bone.
You got your first purple heart,
Only two more and you can go home."

"Just a few more stitches, Marine,
In no time you will heal.
I can even get you back
In time to take the hill."

"Since you're in such a hurry to send me back,
And since they don't go by the book:
Why don't you go in my place
And take a real good look?"

SPIDER HOLE

Choppered to the Car Viet River, a place by the sea,
Nothing but sand dunes, not a safe place to be.
I heard shots on a routine patrol, the guy in front went down,
I hit the sand fast while my eyes searched around.

This is not my kind of action, the jungle's what this grunt knows,
The word came to look for Cong in a one man spider hole.
I got in line, my boots kicked up the sand,
Then Cong opened fire and got another man.

I saw a trap door shut, Cong made a big mistake--
I got around the hole, it was time to seal his fate.
He was ours, we had him made,
He flipped the lid and out flew a grenade.

We ran like hell with only seconds to spare,
The grenade exploded, and Cong was out of there.
He was lucky, smart, and fast today:
While we were eating sand, he just flat got away.

NO BETTER WAY

They try to get in and
We try to keep them out,
That's what war is all about,
To try for political clout.

We want to kill them,
They want to kill you.
This is a war zone,
This is what we're here to do.

They kill for North Vietnam,
We kill for the USA.
This is a waste of men--
Isn't there a better way?

DEATH

Death ain't nothing
But a bullet in the dark
Death is a trip wire
Tied to tree bark

Death is dragging friends
Down a bloody trail
Death is spending 13 months
In massive green hell

Death is being caught in a night ambush,
With bullets all around
Death is a little bamboo viper,
Even he can bring you down

Real death is surviving......

HOW COME

How come this jungle is so thick,
How come this jungle is so green,
How come water appears from an underground stream?

Everyone is dead...

How come sunset in the jungle looks so nice,
How come so many vines hang,
How come people make homes out of bamboo?

Everyone is covered in blood...

How come it rains so many days without stopping,
How come birds sing all at once,
How come the trees have different shapes?

They are taking me away...

How come they invented guns, bullets, and wars?

How come?

CHARLIE'S LAST CHANCE

"Adams to the CP!"
Why would command post want me?
Your orders came in today:
Your headed back to the USA.

I couldn't believe it, was it true?
Am I one of the few to make it through?
I was told to be at the airstrip by first light,
Better not miss this flight.

I could only think of one other guy,
I had to say a last good-bye.
I left the tent, speechless, and headed back to my hole--
After 12 months 3 weeks and a day, at last, I get to go.

They asked how things went,
I told them my time was spent,
We talked until dawn, then to the plane I felt like running,
Then someone yelled, "Incoming!"

I slid for a hole, and it was easy to see
Charlie wanted one last shot at me.
The rounds kept raining, thoughts raced through my head,
"Do your best Charlie, but God, don't let me end up dead."

LAUGHING AND DYING

One minute we're talking and laughing,
An hour later he's in my arms dying.
I tell him, "Hang on man, you'll make it,"
"You're not dying," all the time I know I'm lying.

His leg is blown off.
I reach down pinch off a large vein,
I yell for the corpsman,
This is totally insane.

SQUAD LEADER

I could hear them coming just down the trail--
Sometimes the wait was pure hell.
They were walking into our ambush sight,
Not quite sure how many were headed to fight.

The NVA headed in our direction.
I was hoping they wouldn't stumble in.
Now, it's up to the squad leader, he's put on the spot,
He is the man in charge, he's the one calling the shots.

This was a judgment call, hoped it was never wrong,
What was to be ten, could turn into 50 or 60 Vietcong.
They are close, now, my heart begins to race,
Getting closer and closer, I can almost see their face.

Squad leader carry's a shot gun, no one fires until he blasts.
The squad leader opens fire, or just lets the enemy pass.
Three enemy walking by, there is a weakness in my knees,
Hopefully none of our guys, will have to cough or sneeze.

My count keeps going up, lost track somewhere around ten,
Glad he didn't open up, we only have eight men.
They just keep passing by, not much distance between,
The count is now growing way past nineteen.

Daytime and nighttime, there's no break from this war,
One of the guys kept count, the enemy totaled fifty four.

TRICK WE TRIED

Tying cans to barbed wire
Was a trick we tried.
Rocks inside cans, to rattle,
Should NVA try and sneak inside.

It was a good idea at the time,
An alarm to let us know--
Ran into a small problem at night
When the wind would start to blow.

Suddenly all the cans are rattling,
Don't know what to do,
Wonder if it's the wind,
Or the NVA tying to get at you.

Would shoot off a flare,
Try and light up the sky,
But it would give off our position,
At which time, we could die.

We are just going to have to sit here,
Not really going to know.
First thing in the morning,
Them fucking rocks and cans must go!

HOW DID IT FEEL TO KILL
(YOU ASKED)

Right at day break just before light
NVA came walking in, out of the night.
Our ambush site was good, everyone was awake,
This, was not the time for even the slightest mistake.

Slowly I raised my rifle, careful not to make a sound,
At the same time I forced my elbow, solid into the ground.
Still not knowing, the NVA walked the trail,
Hardly made a sound, they were trained quite well.

This was called pay back, for my friends they had left dead--
Raised my barrel gently, set my sight on this mother fucker's head,
Then we had them, all six were in our view,
No one had to be told, we knew what we had to do.

I pulled back the trigger, felt the kick, as my round slammed his face.
One more NVA removed, from this so-called human race.
They were all dead before they hit the ground,
That was how I wished every ambush could go down.

Now to answer your question, how did it feel,
Many have asked, what it was like to kill?
It felt damned good, this was what we were trained to do--
Better to be looking down at him and not him looking down at you,

It felt good to bring his life to an end,
Maybe he's the one who killed my best friend.
After a while it really didn't mean much,
When it comes to reality I was out of touch.

If you didn't kill him, he would have gladly killed you--
If you were put in my place, what would you do?

PART IV

RETURNING HOME

WELCOME HOME

My year and one month has finally passed and I'm headed home.
I quickly scan the airstrip and see a few men standing alone.
My friends are no longer here, they are all wounded or dead.
The plane for home lands and I hold my helmet fast upon my head.

I am on the plane waiting to fly out of Da Nang,
And I know I will never be the same.
At last the plane takes off and I'm in the air.
I'm thinking about the guys we've left and how none of this is fair.

Now there is no more water beneath me, all I can see is land.
I start to feel good just knowing behind me is Vietnam.
I am so elated knowing I am finally out of the DMZ,
Out of all the brutal battles, the only one to make it home is me.

I was wounded twice in ambush and again on that bloody hill,
But they kept sending me back. To them it was no big deal.
I left the States an innocent teen and now returning a changed man,
I am just another one of the living dead leaving Vietnam.

I waited a long time for this day, but finally I'm on my way.
I know the next stop is the USA.
I took thirty days leave, but my uniform I left behind.
Too many protesters are marching, I can wear it another time.

I conceal my uniform, get on the bus, and head for men's room door.
I had the right to wear it, after all, I made it through the war.
Eight hours later the bus comes to a stop. At last I'm in my home town.
I look outside the window and see protesters marching all around.

I get off the bus, the crowd moves in front of me, and I stand still.
One slaps my face and says "Hey Marine, how many kids did you kill?"
I say "That's a good question, it's really neat,
I never killed more than I could eat!"

He swings hard thinking he could flatten me,
But I put my foot where his manhood had to be.
The police arrive, it didn't take much time,
They throw me in their car and say "Leave, or get beat," the choice mine.

They tell me they don't give a damn that I just came from a war
They say "Don't start any trouble here," as they push me out the door.

WELCOME HOME !

RE-UP

I was called into his office, but wasn't sure what to say,
I knew why I was called in, it was time to re-up today.
I took a chair while he looked at me and gave it to me straight,
Losing a Marine with an outstanding record is something he did hate.

He asked me to re-up for four more years, they needed Marines like me.
Offered me $10,000.00 and sergeant stripes, said how easy this could be.
I really did like the corps and would really like to stay,
He said, "Sign the papers, lets get this out of the way."

I asked, "If I re-up for another four years or so
What would be my duty station, where would I go?"
He said, "You'd get 90 days in the States, guaranteed, my man.
But once that was up, you'd be headed back to Nam."

I told him I didn't want to go back, that I had seen enough war.
He said, "You could return a platoon sergeant, and even up the score."
I would like to make the corps my home for 20 years or so
But, if I had to return to Nam, my answer was surely no.

I must give him credit because he really tried.
I'd only see more death and dying, I can't forget my friends who died.
I couldn't go back over there and he could not change my mind,
If I could have a better duty station, I'd surely sign on the dotted line.

He said, "You are a great combat Marine, and you are needed over there"
But, I told him to fill out my discharge papers as I raised up from the chair,
He said, "Think it over and come back if you decide you want to stay."
I gave him a salute, shook his hand, then turned and walked away.

Three days later I got my papers saying I was again a free man.
I must admit how good it felt, knowing there would be no more Vietnam.
For me, the war was over, and figured I would do rather well--
Little did I know that I just entered the world of another living hell.

I thought once I was off the base
My memory would erase.
But I heard a voice from within
Saying, for some this war will never end.

HOME AGAIN, BIG DEAL

Home now, big deal, I'm back on the block.
Folks invite me over, but they don't want to talk.
Everyone pretends that I never went away,
But when they're with me they don't know what to say.

Next to my bed I keep a knife, and under my pillow a gun.
Mom tells me to leave, she says I'm not the same son.
Even I know I'm different now, that I am not the same--
But I'm sure as hell not the one to blame.

I had to live on the edge for such a long time,
Bit by bit fighting within, until I about lost my mind.
I lived in a hole, ate from a can, and took lives with a gun,
I saw and did too much to come back the same loving son.

The hollowness inside tells me, I'll never be that man again.
Another horror was hunting for body parts of one of my friends.
I am home now, but with a terrified mind--
I could go visit Robert, the war left him blind.

I could drive over to Craig's,
The war took his legs.
I am home now and so is ole' Bill:
He's in a padded cell in the psycho ward, his mind's on the hill.

We are back now, but wrath is the only thing we feel.
Home now, brothers, a very nothing big deal.

THE KID BACK HOME

The Viet Cong may overrun us, that's what I was told.
While the kid back home wonders, if he would ever get cold.
I wear bloodied jungle clothes while the kid back home wears JC Penny.
I worry about dying, while the kid back home worry's if he'll get any.

I carry around the wounded and dead,
While the kid back home gets his car painted red.
My body is covered with a strange jungle rot,
While the kid back home is smoking pot.

I made it home, only God knows how.
All the kids who stayed home are yelling "Peace now!"
I lost a job to that kid who got to stay home.
They said he was better qualified and that he wouldn't roam.

There is so much ignorance and even more fear.
People think Vietnam Vets all do drugs, kill, and drink beer.
So here I stand confused and alone,
I am numb, welcome home.

INTERVIEWS

I went over your job application
But must say, with regret,
I can't hire you because my boss
Doesn't like Vietnam Vets.

I don't know what his problem is,
I think it is just fear
He doesn't want Nam Vets hired,
Or even anywhere near.

I'm sure you can do the job
And would work out just fine,
But to talk any further
Would be wasting your time.

It's a shame they make you look bad,
Even on some TV shows.
The boss doesn't want to deal with that.
Good luck, wherever you go.

BATTLES REAL REWARDS

I was awarded the purple heart
And thought I'd be so proud,
But visible scars from being wounded
Is what stands out in a crowd.

I received the presidential Unit Citation
And the Vietnam Cross of Gallantry,
But all people see are the scars and think
I'm an animal that should be kept in captivity.

I want to share with others
And be proud of these memories,
But looking back at me from the mirror
Is souvenirs from Nam, that others see.

DON'T LISTEN

No one wants to listen to the Vietnam Vet
Because he doesn't want people to ever forget.
Just keep him silent and don't let him speak,
Keep him alone and out on the street.

He might tell truths about things not heard before,
People might think and be horrified when they learn the score.
So many don't believe anything a Vietnam Vet has to say--
When they see him coming, they just go the other way.

If he should ever come over just show him the door,
Just don't give him a chance to talk about the war.
He has to many secrets, dark and grim,
Festering inside, and still haunting him.

Yes, he knows about black markets, kickbacks and graft,
But let's keep him mute and looking bad, he is used to that.

DON'T MEAN MUCH

I went to the flea market
To see what was there.
There was an old vet
Sitting in a wooded chair.

I walked over to the table
To see what he had to sell.
There was a row of medals
Right next to an old bomb shell.

I asked if he was a veteran
From WWII.
He said, "Yes," as I stuck out my hand
And said, "Nice to meet you."

"How can you sell these medals?
You paid a hell of a price in that war."
Teary eyed he said
"Veterans and medals don't mean much anymore."

WAR

I saw blood and gore on the battle fields of red,
And badly wounded, frozen faces, of the dead.
I lived most of the time in a quickly dug out trench
When it monsoons-- under a poncho, alive but with stench.

I tried to write my friend's folks to tell them how he died,
But the only light in the hole to see by was a candle inside.
Trying to write only filled me with fear,
My chest got heavy and I fought back a tear.

The rank war odors all around made me gag.
It was even worse when I loaded body bags
On patrol Mel stepped on a mine,
It could have been me since I was right behind.

Eight friends killed, twelve wounded, all sent home.
I wondered why I was left there all alone.
I was pinned down with a company in bad spot,
Covered in blood, and had my share of jungle rot.

The Cong threw a grenade straight at me--
I didn't move fast enough, and then I couldn't see.
The shrapnel ripped me up, left me bloody and in pain.
I couldn't call out, but screamed inside all the same.

I was in Nam twelve months two weeks and a day.
It took this for them to finally haul me away.
At last I was home thinking there would be no more fear,
But here I am still paying for that fateful year.

Bad dreams and nightmares wake me up in a cold sweat,
I keep reliving the war in Nam, a year I will never forget.

SILENT WARRIORS

They don't say much,
They keep it inside.
These silent warriors are
Stripped of their pride.

Bloody fields and battles
In the mud scarred their minds.
Telling war stories is not how
Warriors pass their time.

They might pick up a piece
Here and there,
But as a rule, the warrior
Will just sit and stare.

Combat warriors
Are few and far between
Painfully speaking,
Of horrors they've seen.

I DON'T CARE

I don't even give a damn
That I'm late to work again,
Not after what I went through
And where I have been.

Mostly, I think about
The Vietnam War
And don't care about anything.
What the hell for?!

I made it home alive,
But there's nothing left inside.
All the feelings I once had,
Now have died.

REMEMBERING

Mom had a dream the night before and called my dad.
She just knew something happened to me and that it was bad.
Dad told her it was just a dream, try and relax and just let it go--
If anything bad happened, they would let us know.

Mom was sitting at the table, it was right at one o'clock.
She noticed a government car coming down the block.
Praying, "Oh God! Don't let them stop. Make them go away."
But inside she knew they would stop here today.

Two men got out of the car dressed in crisp dress blues,
And asked if they could come in, and were sorry to bring bad news.
Her legs were very weak and shaky as she sat down in the chair.
They informed her that her son was badly wounded over there.

When they found out more, they would be sure to let her know.
Sorry they couldn't stay longer but there was a long list to go.
No one will ever know the fears a mother goes through,
Knowing there was absolutely nothing she could do.

The strain was unreal not knowing if I would live or die.
Everyday she would just sit and at some point cry.
This is why she sent me a letter every single day--
She felt a chain of letters would bring me home someday.

There is pain and suffering on both sides of a war.
Someday we would talk again and she could tell me more.
The fear, pain, and suffering so many mothers have done
Starting from the day they take away their sons.

SOMEDAY.....

PHONE CALLS

My picture was in my home town paper
When I was wounded in the war.
It said whose son I was and that I received
The Purple Heart while fighting with the 3/4.

The next day the phone began to ring,
(It was just another mother's dread)
A voice began singing
Your son's dead! Got shot right through the head.

The world is full of people like this,
And fate arranged for her to meet many more.
Another protester told her to be proud
Her son went off to war.

Another call saying, "I won't take much of your time,
I don't want to preach,
Take pride in knowing your son
Is one of the few, the proud, the dead on the beach!"

"Have a nice day."

SATISFIED
(THE BIGGER THEY ARE)

I went in a bar after work
Thought I'd relax and have a beer.
It didn't take long for the hair on my neck
To tell me that trouble was near.

I heard, "What's with the cammie top?
The war ended years ago!
You should drink somewhere else,
You lost the war you know."

Well, I'm five foot seven
And weigh 140 pounds at most,
I turned around to find a man
The size of a telephone post.

He said my cammie top should be yellow
After what happened over there,
But he didn't see my foot come out
From beneath the chair.

First he let out a high pitched scream,
Followed by a low pitched moan--
I always go for the vitals because
I know my foot will hit home.

This man among men stood in front of me,
Leaning on the bar,
So I reached into my pocket for my keys
And headed for the car.

He said something about my mother
And that I was surely dead,
I looked up at the telephone post
And shot a palm thrust to his head.

There was no need to draw blood
Or work up a sweat at all,
I walked away waiting for the sound,
The bigger they are the harder they fall.

NEVER THE SAME

I haven't been the same, ever since the war
Nothing, holds meaning, anymore
SO WHAT?

I carried wounded and dead
And can't get horrid visions out of my head
BIG DEAL!

I'm filled with anger and hate
I need help before it's too late
KEEP QUIET........

My part in Vietnam is over and done
The battles were fought, but no war was won
People didn't care
That we were suffering, and dying, over there
SILENCE.

Some will never understand
The misery we went through, in Vietnam
WHO CARES?

EMOTIONS AND FEELINGS

Where have all the feelings gone,
The ones I had before?
All my emotions are gone,
Ones I had before the war.

It's possible I may never see them again,
No matter how hard I try,
I remember they were nice to have,
When I was alive.

I must have had some good times,
When I was a younger man,
When I felt alive,
But that was before Vietnam.

LOST FEELINGS, LOST FRIEND

I would like to find the happy guy
People say I was before,
They miss the funny, happy, guy
That was sent off to war.

I would stop and smell the roses,
Laid back, but not too much,
I knew the value of laughter,
Crying, and a loving touch.

I am puzzled when they say this,
Since that guy's unknown to me.
He sounds worth knowing more,
Than this guy I seem to be.

I go deep inside myself, to see
If he still exists. God only knows,
How much I want to be that friend,
The one they surely miss.

I want to hold a woman,
Crazy with emotions inside,
I want to look into the mirror
With some form of pride,

I want to be soft and gentle,
Yet, still be a man,
Be that friend of feeling,
The one they lost in Nam.

VETERANS' DAY

Parades on Veterans' Day
Came once a year.
All the proud men
Wanted to cheer

The uniforms WWI, WWII,
Korea, Vietnam.
Once a year, there was pride,
On the face of every man.

Everyone stood around
To shake hands and talk,
Uniforms everywhere,
Up and down the block.

Once a year,
When it rolled around
You'd see Vet's together,
Headed for town.

Now, that the time
Starts to draws near
I'm all dressed up,
But no parade this year.

A "day off" for everyone,
A day to come and go
It's Veterans' Day,
But you would never know.

Once a year!

VIETNAM VET'S TIDE

The ocean roars and the waves roll in
I think about the past and where I've been.
Vietnam is my bloody past,
My relationships and marriages didn't last.

My second marriage came to an end,
I just caught a chill as another wave rolled in.
I wonder if life will ever be normal again
Or turmoil, because of what took place then.

There's something in common with the ocean and I,
A similar mixture can be found, inside.
We can be soft, and easy going
Or compulsory, and tear down everything.

It's hard to be caring and loving when I feel anger and hate.
I made good changes, but they came a little too late.
I could be the greatest guy a girl ever had,
But I feel undeserving, and turn everything bad.

I try hard to persuade her to stay, twice as hard to drive her away
With this indifference I should have died with my friends that day....
I watch the water recede with sparse emotions, I drift back into my shell,
Another wave begins to swell, teary-eyed, I digress back to the time in hell.

THE MIND

I saw the ravages of battle,
It was a laceration of my mind,
A tearing so bad
It cannot be defined.

I keep on fighting,
Even with this mangled rip.
The battle ended,
I wish I could remember none of it.

My mind is frazzled,
Absolutely frayed,
It is, indeed, a high price
Many men have paid.

The mind can give many times,
In a desperate war,
But there comes a time
The mind can bend no more.

GUILT

GUILT...
What we suffer
From twelve months
Of living behind a gun.

SHAME...
What we got
For coming home.

Two gifts,
To sit and ponder
All alone.

We shouldn't feel guilt or shame,
We were fighting in a war.
It doesn't matter,
When your adding up the score.

Our country wants
Vietnam Vets to feel humiliated.
Feelings like this,
Only causes, undying hatred.

DARK AND DEEP

Dark and deep,
Relentless and unknown.
Death, dying,
It sends a chill right to the bone.

Speaking the unspeakable
About fear and dead souls.
Few can speak of what
A combat vet knows.

A little to say,
When speaking of that war.
Madness, insanity,
Sprinkled with blood and gore.

FORGETTING WAR

Forgetting
Is not hard to do,
I can feel better
After a drink or two.

When, drinks are numbered
Three and four,
I care less
About the Vietnam war.

Soon drinks are numbered
Eight, maybe ten,
I pass out, get up tomorrow,
To do it all again.

Forgetting isn't hard,
In fact it's rather easy--
The pain is so deep,

I just drown myself in liquor
This method helps to forget,
All the quicker.

THE NEED

He walked up to the counter and said, "Can I help you son?"
I said, "Yes, I came to buy a knife and a gun."
He said, "What kind do you want, young man?"
I was looking for something like the rifle carried in Vietnam.

He said, "I can't sell a machine gun, but tell you what I'll do--
Take a look at a Mini-14, this pup will give the edge to you."
I held it in my hands, a miniature of the real thing.
I told him I'd take it and heard the cash register start to sing.

He asked if I needed a magazine, maybe a round or two,
I told him to take it easy, I still had shopping to do.
I asked for some 40 round magazines, He said, "They are in the back."
I said, "Get me about four," and pulled some ammo off the rack.

I asked if he had a K-bar? This was my knife of choice.
"I have one under the counter," I noticed an uneasiness in his voice.
I asked, "How much for the jungle sling?"
Since it was his best sell of all, he threw it in for nothing.

I packed up the gear and headed for the door.
He said, "Looks like you're headed off to war!
Why do you need all that, you're no longer in Vietnam?"
"There is a need, for I have seen how inhumane man is to man."

MY HANDS

I look down and see blood on my hands,
A reminder of the time, I spent in Nam.
You can't see it, but to me it's plain as day
The sweat on my forehead, will it go away?

I scrub my hands hard but the blood remains
Then I try soap and water, am I insane?
My hands are sticky like they're covered with glue,
It wont go away, what should I do?

My hands are red, and sticky, and starting to smell.
God, please take away this mind-bending hell.
Who can I talk to, of such an event?
If I bring this up, I'll wonder where everyone went.

If I see a Doctor to discuss this bloody smell,
I will soon be headed for a padded cell.
There must be something that can be done--
Until then I put gloves on, and hope the blood won't run.

WON IN WAR

Insanity....
Something I never experienced before
Mental disorder....
Something won in war

I became a mad man, a maniac
A psychopath, on the run
Only nineteen
But stayed alive with a gun

Gradually I became demented
It spread like disease
I joined the creatures
Snuck through the jungle on my knees

I wound up on a psychiatric ward
Delirious, going mad, yes
The fighting is over, but when my mind's
War is over, is anyone's guess

EXPLAIN TO HER

Last night my wife asked
What was going through my head.
I was reliving savage battles
And seeing faces of the dead.

She wonders
What is wrong with me,
No matter how hard I try,
I can't make her see.

I don't know where to start
And I also fear the end,
I need to help this woman,
My wife, lover, my friend.

I'm afraid the fact is,
That I may never adjust--
Flashbacks, nightmares,
Anger, hate and mistrust.

There was so much
I lost in the war,
I'll never be the guy
I was before.

I want to let her in,
But keep pushing her away,
This contradiction goes on,
Day after day.

I fear letting her get close,
But I desperately need a friend,
Like living in a trap, God knows,
I don't want her falling in.

A POEM I WOULD LIKED TO HAVE RECEIVED

I spend days inside your head
Looking at the things you dread,
It burdens our days and taints our bed.

I can't erase the memory of war
That makes you pace the floor
Nor can I shield you from the gore.

I can only hold the flame
Sometimes, take on all the blame
And fend off guilt, and needless shame.

I promised I would share your strife
When I said I'd be your wife
Hold onto this, because I meant it, for life.

JULY FOURTH FLASHBACKS

Polluting the sky with rockets, they fill the air
The flashing light and blasts I hear
Put me in a cold sweat as I drift back there

THE WAR

I'm sweating on the outside, but icy cold within
My mind forces me back, to where I have been

VIETNAM

I try to escape by pulling the covers over my head,
In bed, I clearly see torn and mangled faces
Of the wounded and dead

FLASHBACKS

My mind is full of stories that I cannot tell
Horrors from the jungles of hell,
Make me wonder if I'll ever get well

SOMEBODY HELP ME!

FLASHBACKS

It's quiet now, and I soothe myself,
It's just a mind playing game
It'll be okay, it can't cause pain
I'll hold back these feelings of going, slowly insane

VIETNAM

ANYBODY, HELP ME!

FLASHBACKS

DAMN DREAMS

I really didn't think I'd ever have to kill
Still hoping, I gradually topped the hill.

PREPARED

The village was half empty, most had to desert
Then, unexpected bullets were forced to the earth.

TRAINED

I swiftly swung my rifle at a VC by the hut.
Bucked my shoulder hard and shot him in the gut.

DYING

He dropped to his knees, with pain coating his face.
Blood ran from his chest, through his fingers, and every place.

VERY VIVID

He fell face forward, with a thud he hit the ground.
Twisting, rolling, screaming, oh, that inhumane sound.

It may be over, but it's not through.
The memory comes back, no matter what I do.

DAMN DREAMS!

TO SLEEP NOT DREAM

I lay down and am at last, asleep.
The covers move, I feel something at my feet,
A chill moves up my legs, now it's at my side,
It's a chill no more, but a friend that died.

Mangled and torn, covered in blood,
His stiffened fingers, claw at my sheet.
I try to remain calm,
He opens his mouth releasing a death stench
And says, "Thank you, for writing Mom."

His body is frozen, incredibly cold.
He talks of death, and things that never are told.
He moves away slowly,
His friends are calling and he must go.

The bed actually moves, I saw it in the night!
I bolt to the bathroom, slam the switch for light,
Stare in the mirror at my cheek, it's bloody red:
God, he kissed me, my friend who is dead.

Now, a dilemma, two choices of dread
Stay awake forever.....or go back to bed!

HEY, GOD

Why do they say
"For God and country" to fight?
I just received a draft notice,
"Hey, God, you forgot to write."

Dead and wounded
All over that hill,
"Hey, God, I thought you said,
(Thou shalt not kill)"

Who do I ask for forgiveness,
You or Uncle Sam?
He is just a poster,
You're out of sight, my Man.

No one said
If this was right or wrong,
I don't even know
Where I belong.

Am I headed
For heaven or hell?
All I can do is wonder
Will I ever get well.

Hey, God, we have to meet,
Then You can dry my tears,
And tell me why I had to suffer
Thirteen months and twenty years.

THE DAYMARE

Death, something to face everyday
Make a mistake, it's the price you pay

There's prolonged death, quick death
Lost limbs, crippling, and some even blind
Noises, voices, and visions
Careful, don't lose your mind

A friend dead here, another dead there
I want to wake from this bad dream
Too bad, I am awake, it's a daymare

NAM VET FEELING BAD

A feeling just came over me, but there's nothing I can do,
I'm feeling mean, bad and just a hint of blue.
I reach into the closet, yes, it's still hanging there,
I put on my cammie top, we're going out for air.

Just one hour earlier, I had on a shirt and tie,
Now I'm feeling mean and bad and care less if I die.
Why do these feelings overcome me, suddenly I just don't care,
I go to the closet and take my mini-14 out of there.

I know I'm looking for trouble and I know things aren't right,
But I am dressed to kill and looking for a fight.
This really isn't me, this is someone born of war--
I'd like to leave him, but I can't, I've tried so many times before.

I try to keep "Born of War" in check, at times he'll let out a warrior's yell,
He needs to be given a little time; remember, he has been through hell.
He thinks he's in the jungle and he thinks life is a scream,
The time to watch out, is when he's feeling mean.

"Born of War" is part of me and I am part of him
There is no way to split us up because we are the same within.

SILVER STAR

"Hey dude! what's happening? I heard you made it home."
I tried to figure out who's voice was on the phone.
"Hey man it's Leo, I was a month ahead of you."
I lost track of him in boot camp, now he calls out of the blue.

"Give me three hours, I'm on my way down.
"I'd really like to see you and we can hit the town."
We found a bar and sat at a booth for two.
Leo looked at me and asked, "What's new?"

We drank and talked, it was a really nice bar.
Leo was wounded twice and received the Silver Star.
I asked how he got it and slowly his story began.
He said they were at a listening post and got overran.

His hands began to shake and tears filled his eyes--
The only one left standing, they killed every one of his guys.
He said after that happened, he was never the same;
Nine months in the bush, sent home, for fear he'd gone insane.

He said he couldn't stop stabbing the dead NVA,
Tried to make sure they were dead so he wouldn't get blown away.
He said he didn't want to go on living-- too much in his head.
He said every night when asleep he saw faces of friends laying dead.

I told him this would pass, the mind takes time to heal.
We finished drinking our beers, then picked up the bill.
I told him we could meet and talk, I'd help get this off his chest.
He put his arm around me and said, "You are the best!"

Three days later I got my mail, then walked back to my car.
I opened the little box sent to me and inside found his Silver Star.
There was a note attached, "Keep this my friend, won't need it anymore.
Sorry, can't handle it ....a bullet will put an end to my war."

Leo

(The Silent Warrior)

THE SERVICE

I lifted the shining brass bar,
Step by step, I walked the coffin closer to the hole.
The box wasn't very heavy
And there were only a few more steps to go.

I slowly draped a flag over the box,
The priest began to talk,
"He was a fine man,
Who became quiet upon returning home--

A good man, but by choice, he remained alone.
We are not to judge, why, he took his life the other day
Let us bow our heads and pray.
Oh God, take care of this young Marine, up in that sky of blue.

Be patient, we are hoping he can talk to You, Almighty God,
We know he made it home from the war, ten years to this day,
He couldn't seem to let it go.
Still, it was the war that took his life away."

At last, the service ended
And I stood there with the rest
A chill shot through me and I heard a voice say,
"I'll see you my friend, you are the best."

PEACE AT LAST.......

GOOD-BYE

I said "Hey, bartender! Over here"
"Hey, man, bring me another beer"

He asked, "What's the occasion
I'd really like to know"

I said "You wouldn't understand
Another silent warrior had to go"

COMBAT VET

I look into his eyes and it sends a chill down my spine.
I know that look well, and can tell he's had a rough time.
They say eyes are the doorway to the soul,
The things I see there, most people don't know.

At times he frightens me because he knows no fear.
When he speaks he knows, I'm the only one who hears.
I'm his only friend and he knows me very well,
There's pain and death in his eyes, from time he spent in hell.

He stands before me now with agony written on his face.
I woke up from dreaming of bloody bodies all over the place.
As I look into the mirror he leans in close, and I can read his mind;
In a panic I throw water, because I know I'll see him another time.

HAPPY TO SEE YOU

Here I am again, your night time dread.
I'm so happy to see you finally came to bed.
Don't resist me, and do not try to fight--
The days may be yours, but I own the night.

It's time to take a journey while you sleep.
We are going back again to the dark and deep.
You will get no rest there's only time to dream
About all the past horrors you've lived and seen.

I plan to haunt you night after night,
Until you take your sorrow and make it right.
You must learn to forgive and let it all go
Or every night there will be a one man show.

You can roll back and forth side to side,
But there is no where to run, no where to hide.
You can break into a cold sweat and claw the sheet,
Better make amends or every night we will meet.

It is very hard to forgive and easy to hate,
That's why you deal with me whenever it's late.
Just hold onto suffering with a strong grip on pain.
Well, please hang on, I really enjoy this game.

Don't blame me for these night terror and bad dreams.
It's your fault you wake up in a sweat with loud screams.
I couldn't get into your mind if you dealt with your fears,
So until you do I will be with you, for years and years.

CONSCIENCE

I'm your conscience,
That's my name.
I make you feel guilt
And even more shame.

I am buried deep,
In the back of your mind,
And I can come to life
At any time.

I will always be with you,
Even at the end.
I'm your worst enemy,
But could also be a friend.

I can make you happy
And I can make you mad.
Since I keep a recording of
Good and bad times you've had.

You have no control
Over anything I do,
Good or bad memories
Is really up to you.

JUDGMENT DAY

I stood before the Lord bathed in a radiant light,
And asked about my time on earth, I thought I did all right.
"Did I uphold Your commandments, how did I treat my fellow man?"
I was worried I'd go to hell for what happened in Vietnam.

I admitted I wasn't perfect but did what I had to do.
I said, "I was ordered to go fight for my country, the flag, and You."
He said He watched that war, from His throne in heaven above,
Saw me raise my right hand and swear an oath, for my country's love.

God said, "Your leaders lied, they made too many die in vain."
He said, "It wasn't right to make you fight and swear an oath in My name."
He glared at me from where He sat and looked down as if in shame,
Then tore a page from the book of life, it was the page with my name.

I saw lightening and heard thunder, as He threw my name on the floor.
God said, "You sinned my son, by taking part in this horrible war."
The sky turned black and roared with rage as He raised high His hand
"Now it's time for judgment," He commanded, "for your sins in Vietnam."

As the heaven's crashed and lightening flashed, I bolted upright in the bed.
I was trembling and screaming, bathed in sweat from visions of hell in my head.
Outside the rain was pouring down and I heard a voice as I paced the floor,
"My son, you were condemned to hell when they sent you off to war."

"I can see the pain and suffering you've endured, is far worse than that in war.
Faith in Me has purged your sins, you're forgiven and welcome at my door."

NIGHTMARES OF VIETNAM

What is wrong, nothing seems right
I'm still doing battle, night after night.
I toss and turn and roll around in bed
I won't sleep until they are all dead.

NIGHTMARES

They were killed in Vietnam, it should have ended there
But I see these dead faces floating around through the air.
Even after twelve years, they come back to me this way
I don't think they will ever leave, they just want to stay.

I WON'T SLEEP

I was told when I killed them, their souls were left to roam
Because the way they died leaves them with no place to go.
Now there are all of these wandering dead souls
Who decided to follow me home, and will not leave me alone.

AFRAID TO SLEEP

It's so hard to live with night after night.
How can this be fair how can this be right
How long can I last with these visions in my head
Killing and sleeping with faces of the dead.

NIGHTMARES OF VIETNAM

WHAT WOULD THEY SAY

They are the silent warriors
Lying in their graves
All these silent warriors
Were once so brave.

I wonder why not many people
Show up anymore
To pay tribute to these men
That died in the war.

They are the silent warriors,
This is the price they had to pay
If only they could speak now
I wonder what they'd say.

Would they say they were proud
To give up their life,
Leaving behind their families,
Some perhaps a wife.

Would they say we're proud to die
For the red, white, and blue,
Would they be proud
To give up their life for you?

Would they say they were happy
That our country is still free
Or would they ask,
"Why have you forgotten me?"

CHILD OF DREAD

I'm still awake and it's half past two.
I'm afraid to sleep, they have haunting to do.
I open my eyes and now it's a quarter to three,
Out of the darkness I see eyes staring back at me.

These eyes move closer to my bed,
Once again I fight this night time dread.
Lifeless eyes frozen in time,
And an outreached hand right next to mine.

In the darkness there's a face of a child
My blood pumps hard, and my heart runs wild.
Suddenly the room is damp, musty, and smelly,
A lifeless form asks me for more jelly.

She said the sweet jelly took away her bitter death,
She gets close enough so I can feel her breath--
Years ago the NVA gunned her down
And her lost soul just follows me around.

In her hand is a C-ration can,
The one I had given her that day in Vietnam.
She placed her dead, cold hand into mine
And said she'd be sure to visit me another time.

I woke up, or was I even asleep?
There is no difference
Once I enter the dark and deep.

BIG WORDS

PSYCHOTHERAPY---Yes, I had that.

PSYCHOTHERAPIST--- One who tries to tell you just where it's at.

PSYCHOANALYZE--- Yes, they have tried that too.

PSYCHOTIC--- That's the end result.

That is what they think of me......

PUSH COMES TO SHOVE

In the bar he asked me,
"What happened to your face?"
That was all it took
And I flashed back to another place.

"Hey, where did you get that scar?
I'm talking to you man."
Instantly I was in combat mode,
As if I was back in Vietnam.

He pushed on my arm,
So I stood and turned around,
"You better answer me man,
Or I will put you down."

He took a swing
But I did an outward block,
Then slapped him upside the head,
I didn't want to talk.

It seemed to make him madder,
And his face turned scarlet red.
I blocked a kick for my groin
And slapped him upside the head.

He took another kick
I just stepped aside, said "what the heck,"
I put my hand into a rigid knife edge
And shot it hard right to his neck.

I really don't like fighting
Or making people hurt,
But when push comes to shove,
I'll die before I eat any more dirt.

HELL'S OWN DREAM

I was in boot camp just seconds ago,
Awakened with a start.
It was the beginning, but I know
The loathsome sequence by heart.

I'm reluctant, but so weary,
I'm forced to return to bed for rest.
In this ongoing nightmare,
I fly back to Nam again to be put to a test.

I can smell the odors in the air,
And feel the fear pounds through my veins.
I'm sobbing as I spring upright,
Then pace the floor, feeling all the old pains.

The newest kind of enemy fatigue
Drags me back and I must have sleep.
Soon, I'm past the dreams and nightmares,
Straight to the dark and deep.

I go to the worst degree of dreaming,
A realm most people never reach.
These night terrors I endure,
Only atrocities of war can teach.

Faces, places, killing, dying, blood and mud,
Are flooding my mind,
I fight to get conscience so I can escape
The mad scene and leave it behind.

I'm locked in for the duration,
And no one else hears the screams
Of a ghoulish voice,
"Jack, all are dead now, it's just you and me."

We do battle, death and I,
Until the night terror has it's way.
Only the dawn can let me out,
I'm not really alive to face another day.

WHO WILL I MEET TONIGHT

Every night again and again
I dream of a rifle pointed at me and me killing him.
Every night (it never fails)
I journey back to that 13 months in hell.

I go to bed and don't want to dream,
And wake up in a sweat followed by a scream.
I close my eyes and clutch the sheet
Never knowing who I will meet.

Will it be faces of the men I left dead
Or friends that died, next to my bed.
It's nighttime fear and nighttime dread--
Will I be visiting or fighting with the night time dead?

I turn out the light and wonder who I will meet
When I once again enter the dark and deep.

URGE TO KILL

At last, I'm home from the war.
But now things are much harder than before;
There were no laws on the front line
I would take his life, before he took mine.

Now I'm left with this urge to kill.
It hits me in the stomach and makes me ill.
A killer, slaying and destruction was what I did best--
Now, I'm home overnight, expected to put the past to rest.

The order to forget won't easily come
After butchery, bloodshed and living by the gun.
A man slayer and executioner, triggered off by deaths blow
Then forty eight hours later, I'm home and told to let it go.

It's hard to suppress life's injustices, and I try to keep it in.
I worry how my training will just surface again.
What will happen when I can't fight that urge to kill any more?
I'm terrified that my reaction will be far worse than that in war.

NEVER HEAL

There is no more laughing, only crying.
The dead are all around, there are screams from men dying.
The eyes that show death are in the empty shell of a man--
These silent warriors who fought in Nam.

There were no parades when we came home
So many of us returned, but are still feeling alone.
Some people wonder and many ask why
58,479 men and women had to die.

There are those who still wonder and will even say
What about our POW's and our MIA's?
Obviously the war isn't over there are too many loose ends.
Everyone was whisked out of there like gale force winds.

Ten years of war left many scars, that even time will never heal.
And our country acts like it didn't happen, as if it's no big deal.

GETTING LATE

I can't take much more,
It feels like time is getting late,
So once again I load six chambers
In my bedside 38.

Why do I bother with six,
When all it will take is one?
I guess it's just another habit
Of living by the gun.

I lay there and as always,
I can't stop thinking about war.
So I cock the pistol and look
Straight down the bore.

If I'd just do it now
It would end nightmares and pain.
It seems there's little to lose
And much more to gain.

In so many ways I'm already dead,
So why not cash it in.
It is so hard to keep going,
After where I've been.

I'm convinced that the thing to do
Is so clear to see,
But an inner voice says people
Love and care about me.

Just when I think I've got it figured out,
And everything feels right
Another voice asks
"Should I pull off the round or turn out the light?"

ANY IDEA

I spent 13 months living in a hole and eating from a can.
Do you have any idea, what this will to a man?
I killed the enemy and watched friends get blown away
Do you have any idea what that is like, day after day?

I couldn't even bath or shower in over a month or two--
Do you have any idea what this kind of living will do?
There was really no safe area for the fighting man,
Not for anyone who had to serve combat in Vietnam.

I had to live every day and night in fear.
Do you have any idea, living this way for over a year?
I was forced to fight a war Americans didn't think was right.
Do you have any idea what this is like?

I found that my own country wouldn't welcome me home.
Do you have any idea what it's like to feel so alone?
Even other Vet organizations didn't want to see our face.
They figured they were first, while our war took second place.

We fought, we bled, and so many died
For a country who couldn't show us any pride.
Do you have any idea why we're treated this way?
I guess it is just a double price we have to pay.

THE HOUR

I was scheduled to go to the hospital to see the Doc.
I walked into his office, but couldn't find words to talk.
He knows I'm having trouble, and drove 60 miles to get there
But now that I'm in his office, I just sit and stare.

There is only one hour to get things off my chest
So I tell him about my nightmares, and how I can't get any rest.
I tell him how pissed off I am for the way my country treated me,
And tell him that I'm thinking about how sweet revenge would be.

I tell him that I'm a trained killer, but that's not needed anymore.
I ask him "Why didn't they retrain me, when I came back from war?"
I am still trained to kill with a rifle, a knife, or even my bare hands.
That's what happens to leftover warriors, home from Vietnam.

My fuse is short and I'm filled with anger, rage, and hate.
I ask if there is something he can do, before it's too late.
I ask if he'd just give me some insight, as I reach over for my cup
But he looks at his clock, then says, "Sorry son your hour is up."

MASTER DREAMER

Here comes the master dreamer,
Kill him and toss him into the well (Gen 37:19)
Joseph was hated an envied for his dreams
Of the future they could tell.

I'm a master dreamer, too,
But my dreams recount horrors of my past,
Haunting seeks my days and nights
By the long shadow they cast.

Joseph's night time vision came true
And he was a king,
But mine only mean a death,
A mental killing.

I try to forget the misery,
You terrify me with nightmares (Job 7:14)
This was Job's lament,
He knew not of night terrors.

God speaks in dreams and night visions
When deep sleep falls on men.
He opens their ears, in times like these,
To give them wisdom and direction.

Is that it, Lord, try to make me see
And hear some type of special instruction;
So I can rest and quit this fight, find peace,
Be released from war's destruction?

Is this the reason I write so much and
Put my Vietnam experience in verse:
The Master plan for this dreamer
Is to alleviate wars curse?

Let those who read *The Promise*,
Understand and learn to cope.
In peace I will sleep and rest, You, alone
Have settled me in hope (Psalms 4:9-10).

ONE YEAR LATER

I walked through a grave yard
Quiet and alone
By all the markers,
Until I found the right head stone.

I asked why this happened
To the only friend I had.
I was upset, but thought the choice
May not be all that bad.

I told him I was still out here
Doing everything I could.
He couldn't answer,
But I knew he understood.

I thanked him for the Silver Star,
Said I would never let it go,
Promised to someday write a story,
So that the world would know.

Leo, another one of many who couldn't
Handle the aftermath of Vietnam,
Everyone would like Leo,
And now, I hold his story in my hand.

APOLOGIES

Dear Mom and Dad,

I want you to know, the war did a lot of damage to me,
I'm sorry I didn't turn out the way you hoped I'd be.
I'm sorry for the fits of anger and for the fits of rage,
I feel like an animal that should be locked in a cage.

I wanted you to be proud of me, so I went off to war,
I'm sorry I wasn't returned to you, the son I was before.
Since I went to hell and back there's little left inside--
Forgive me for the pain I've caused, sometimes I wish I'd died.

I know I don't keep in touch very much, that's just the way I am.
I don't think it's anything you've done, it's only been since Vietnam.
I really wish I could talk to you, but I just don't know what to say,
The pain goes so deep I don't think it will ever go away.

I rarely feel warmth in my heart, and don't know how to act when I do.
I know when I finally do get this feeling, it's when I'm thinking of you.
I'm sorry I didn't get this to you, so dad could have read it before he died,
So please take this with you, to him, when once again you are at his side.

Your Son,

Jack

JUNKIE HOOKED ON WAR

They beat me, trained me, made me their whore--
Soon I became another junkie, hooked on war.
They made me a killer, one of the very best,
I always stood out among all the rest.

I was stripped of my youth, yet still not quite a man.
Shoot them, kill them, rip out their throats with my hands.
Brainwashed to kill, this was mans inhumanity to man--
Survival, the name of the game, when I was in Vietnam.

Frenchie, Hefner, and Chevez were all lost on the same day,
But, those mother fucker's paid, I quit counting my killing's of the NVA.
My days of youth are over, no caring, no emotions, and no heart of gold,
Just a junkie hooked on killing, with lust for blood, and a heart gone cold.

Then they killed my friends Byrd, Johnson, and Pa Pa Brown--
I was no longer killing, but also burning villages down.
I was kept in the jungle longer than any other unit in the war.
I no longer care, I'm just a junkie out to even the score.

I'm hooked on killing, and empty shell inside,
Just another jungle beast leaving the enemy no where to hide.
Got a letter from mom, full of love and care--
I told her not to write, anymore as long as I was there.

Poor woman doesn't know her teenage son has nothing left inside,
I might be better if someone just wrote and told her I died.
Home, mother, brother, what the fuck is that?
I'm a junkie hooked on killing, show me where the enemy is at.

Hooks, Stringer, and Parpala all died last night,
To bad they walked into an NVA ambush site.
One by one, my real family is dying--
We stack our dead and there's not one Marine crying.

I know what they're thinking, why isn't there even one tear?
We want revenge, to kill, that fix, we'll be here over a year.
We toss more of our dead, best, friends into a stack--
Don't sweat it brothers, there will be a pay back.

RETURNING HOME ★ 120

We jump from the choppers ordered to take the hill,
Caught in a crossfire, they kill Riggs, Shawley, even got Wild Bill.
I break into a rage, then black out and about lose my mind--
Everything turns into a haze and I can't even account time.

It's a feeling I have, I just know I can't die!
I can't explain it, so don't bother asking me why.
Next I'm running full speed ahead,
Behind me is a trail of blood and the NVA I left dead.

I'm all over the hill running around,
Finding the NVA and gunning them down.
I snap back to reality and find a place to hide,
Suddenly two guys drop right by my side.

They are laughing and telling me that I'm insane.
I remember nothing, not even their names.
Now I feel fear and I start to shake,
Knowing inside this war is a mistake.

For some reason, I no longer want to kill,
But I have no choice, so we advanced up the hill.
The blood mixes with mud to an off colored red,
Not one of the old bunch is left, they're all wounded or dead.

I've been here over a year and I just want to go home
Fuck, I have never felt so terribly alone!
We ran into a concrete bunker, all over the hill guys are dying,
As for taking the bunker, no one is even trying.

I rub my cross, my St. Christopher, too.
Then say, "Fuck it, Lord, sure hope I end up with you."
I grab the flame thrower man and say "let's move ahead,"
Then we slowly crawl over our wounded and dead.

I turn on his tanks, he gets on his knees
And blasts his flames, out through the trees.
I will admit he did his very best,
But he took two bullets right in the chest.

He slammed back into me and now my rifle's lost,
It's time to retreat at all cost.
I take his tanks off and roll him for a hole,
What a big surprise, little did I know.

I looked at the bunker and saw an NVA--
He smiled, pulled the pin, and tossed his grenade my way.
The flame thrower's safe in the hole, so I dive to join him there,
But the grenade goes off, catching me in mid-air.

My god, the pain, the deep burning inside!
As 42 pieces of burning steel rip into my hide!
"Lord," I cry, "What has happened to me?"
"God, I'm blind, I can't see!"

I feel my face, with all the tiny pieces of steel.
I lay with the rest, bleeding and blind on the hill.
I ask God to let me die, I can't go home blind,
"Let me be, Lord, please leave me behind."

But the Corpsman drags me down the hill to a safer place,
It was Snyder, and I ask him about my face.
He tells me nothing, so I ask again, to tell me what he knows.
He said I would live, if he can patch up all the fucking holes.

He'd patch the bleeders, the rest would have to wait.
I lay there wondering, if this is to be my fate.
I ask for something to make the pain go away,
He said "Sorry, Jack, ran out of that early today."

I really did like Snyder, he was one hell of a guy.
Too bad three days later, it was his turn to die.
One chopper was leaving with wounded and dead,
I heard it get blown out of the air, just overhead.

I feel myself tossed on a chopper, now leaving this place--
My hands are tied down, so I couldn't pull the steel from my face.
The chopper tries to get us to the USS Repose,
But there's too much fog, where the carrier is at, nobody knows.

The pilot says we have to head for Phu Bai
We're running out of gas, and must go before we all die.
Someone starts pulling at my clothes
Then puts me on a stretcher, placing something over my nose.

Don't know where I'm going, just bounced around--
I hear screaming voices, I can hear every little sound.
Now I can sense there is a lot of people all around,
My clothes are cut off me and tossed to the ground.

I hear a voice say "Can you hear me, son, are you awake?"
I say "Yes sir, and lay there waiting for my fate."
He pulls at the medivac card around my neck,
To see how I was wounded, a way to check.

"It says here, you were hit by a grenade on hill 174,"
"We have to work fast, son, there are more at the door."
The bandages were removed from my head
Then I heard someone say, "Move this Marine out, he's dead."

I ask, "How bad is my face, will I ever again see blue skies?"
"Don't know son, but won't tell you lies,"
Then he yells, "Give this kid a shot, make his pain go away!"
"I can't believe you've been suffering all day."

Then I feel needles going in here and there--
Soon, there's no more pain, felt anywhere.
Then a voice says, "I have to start digging all this metal out,"
"If you need to, just go ahead, scream and shout."

He began pulling out the steel, I tried to take it like a man.
I heard each piece of steel, as he dropped it in the pan.
The pain was just too much to take and I had to give in,
So I laid there yelling, "Mother fucker!" over and over again.

I heard the voice say, "Found a bleeder, give me a clamp!"
"Let's start on his face, move the lamp!"
The voice said, "Can you see this light?"
I said, "I can't see anything, will I be all right?"

RETURNING HOME ★ 123

The voice said "I'm doing everything that I can do,"
"The rest is up to God, and you."
I can feel three people, sewing up my holes--
I lay there thinking, what the fuck, guess that's the way it goes.

The pain killer wears off and I want to scream and shout--
Then hit with enemy rockets, there's no one to help this blind guy out.
I ripped out my IV, screaming, to anyone that I can't see!
At last, someone grabbed and took hold of me.

Waiting in the hole, there's nothing I can do
A rocket hit too close to the bunker, now I'm ruptured, too.
After a few days of praying, I could see once again.
That's when I asked the Doc, "What's with my skin?"

The Doc said, "Sorry son, flash burns never go away,"
"Your skin pigmentation will always look that way."
I look at my arms, legs, and again at my face,
There are stitches everywhere, what a fucking waste!

Guess it was just another one of this wars curse.
What the hell, I had seen much worse.
I was grateful, at least I wasn't blind,
That had really been messing with my mind.

If this is the worse to happen, I guess I'll survive.
The Doc said, I was damn lucky to even be alive.
Now it's time to start playing the game:
I called it focus, a way to deal with the pain.

It was to soon for medication, so I'd just focus on the pain,
Slowly move it away, or I would surly go insane.
I looked at the others with missing arms, legs and eyes,
Such a waste of so many young guys.

I kept to myself, stayed in my world all alone
With thoughts going through my head, I might get to go home.
The Doc came to tell some of the guys, they were headed home,
But when he got to my cot and looked at my chart, as I lay alone.

RETURNING HOME ★ 124

He asked how I felt, I said "All right I guess, what's the deal?"
"Sorry Marine, in a couple of days, your headed back for that hill."
The tears start building up inside,
But I don't let it out, I focus and hide.

The stitches are out and I'm issued new gear,
Back to the bush isn't what I want to hear.
It takes three Purple Hearts to get out of the war--
What the fuck, I only needed one more!

I keep getting hit, and they keep sending me back.
I must be born under the sign of shit, that's it, Jack.
I wonder how much I can take, before my mind gives out?
Here comes my chopper, guess I'll soon find out.

Every man has his limit, it's only a matter of time.
I'm not real sure, but I think I've already lost my fucking mind.
I am just another whore
A junkie, they got hooked on killing, and war.

THE TATTOO ARTIST

My days are plagued and so are my nights
From many battles of my past and fire fights
Scars on my body where fragments and bullets went through
Are very visible, but I don't know what to do.

A master tattoo artist turns my scars into pictures, one night in a dream,
As if my skin were a big screen, scars of war no longer mean a thing.
The next day I went to a church asking God to help me find this man,
Merlin of magic, to turn scars and burns into beauty, help erase Vietnam.

Then one day as I drove along, I saw a sign that read "Tattoo,"
The vision of a cross appeared next to it, was my request coming true.
I turned my car around, not really knowing why,
A heaviness within my chest just wouldn't let me pass by.

I walked up to the door to a sign that read, "Come In!"
He didn't turn around, and said, "I've been waiting for you, my friend."
He said the Master had a reason, he reached down and touched my heart,
"Told me you were coming to look over some of my works of art."

Slowly he turned, yet still remaining in his chair--
I was stricken by all the beautiful art he had placed around everywhere.
He said, "I understand you need help, that's why you were sent to me."
"Don't be ashamed of scars from war, remove your shirt and let me see."

I said, "I feel reluctant in doing what you say
I only hope you can look at me, without turning away."
Taking off my shirt he ran his hand across my chest, my flash burns and scars,
And said, "I see a panther guarding a castle, a backdrop of meteors and stars."

I was taken back by what he said to me,
For the burns and scars he didn't see.
I thought, for the first time I may no longer have to hide.
I sat a bit taller, at long last, feeling some pride.

No more words were spoken, he tossed back his long braided hair,
Pointed to his mystical table, "Please have a seat over there."
He carefully drew an outline on my chest.
The vision I had of the cross, told me I had the best.

He told me it may hurt a bit, as he started on the stars.
I replied, "It would hurt a lot less than how I got the scars."
Then I heard a fine low hum,
The master's hand approached with his finely tuned gun.

Suddenly, I felt a bit of a sting,
Nothing new to this combat Marine.
It felt good to be with the master tatoo artist and I was in a hurry to begin ,
For I knew he was erasing bad memories of the places I had been.

He said, "You fought for God and country, you put up one hell of a fight,
I'm pleased the higher powers introduced us in a dream you had last night."
I wasn't about to ask how he knew,
And after two hours he said, "I guess we are through."

He handed me a mirror, it was breathtaking seeing all the meteors and stars,
The panther, the castle, a waterfall, and no more burns and scars.
I told him this was outstanding, and we had lots more to do.
He laid down his magic gun and said, "My friend, I'll always be here for you."

I told him my scars and burns there are so many--
But he stopped and said "My friend, I have yet to see any."
I began to walk away feeling proud and warm
I turned and asked his name he replied, "My friends, they call me *Storm*."

Take care brother, as you know
We have a long way to go!

JD

STANDARD ANSWERS

We kept in touch
When we came home,
This way neither one of us
Would be alone.

Some years later
He became very sick,
The doctor didn't know
What to think of it.

He began to drop weight,
Inside he began to rot,
Needless to say
His health was totally shot.

He didn't enjoy much
Of his younger life,
Leaving behind
Two kids and a wife.

Slow death from Agent Orange,
Once dropped from the air,
Many face the same thing,
The vets that fought over there.

We are told Agent Orange
Doesn't cause cancer
Until we are all dead
This will be standard answer.

DISABLED

He was doing all right until his check came in the mail.
They cut his disability, VA said he was now doing well.
He really wasn't doing good, he really was a mess,
But the VA wasn't going to let him rest.

He tried to fight them, of course, at his cost,
And the end result was that he lost.
So what is left after they take this away,
Can't pay bills and there's no place to stay.

I know what he did, he was close to me.
He took all the medication he had, died of an OD.
Some think vets have it easy, they have it made,
But that disability is for the price that they paid.

They can cut disability any time,
Just do it without reason or rhyme.
The sad part of this is, I want you to hear
They keep doing this to vets year after year.

Seldom will you read about it, it's something I dread,
They cut disability and some of my friends turn up dead.

THE MORNING

In the morning they ask if I slept all right,
Of course I did, fire fight after fire fight.
They want to know if I slept or not,
Last night I tended my wounds and jungle rot.

They want to know if I slept good or poor,
All night long I fought the endless war.
They want to know if I had a flashback,
How can I flashback when Vietnam's where I am at.

They are trying to help and they're doing their best,
It's not their fault that I can't rest.
Every night is the same, every night I battle the Cong,
Every night I kill and kill, watch friends die all night long.

I can tell you in the morning I had bad dreams last night.
Forgive me, if I seem on edge and uptight--
Forgive me, if I snap at you,
It's tough being up all night and killing's all I do.

Bear with me if I don't seem right,
But this shit goes on night after night.

PSYCHE WARD

Back on the Psyche ward, this time, the 5th floor
Again to battle the stress, anxiety, pressure left over from war.
It's like I'm falling apart and I don't know what to do,
Battle after battle fought in brown pajamas, and sometimes blue.

I have seen blood on my hands, hear voices in my head,
Voices aren't bad, but they're from friends I lost they're dead.
At least the doctor's don't think I'm insane.
The doc talks kind of funny and has a foreign name.

Then there is Geri, her heart's as pure as gold,
Never need to ask for anything, she never has to be told.
Why am I still a mess why am I still paying the price,
Why is it I can't change, turn into something nice?

I dream of the blood and guts and grave rats in my bed,
Sometimes I wake up screaming shaking sweat from my head.
My stomach's tied in knots, my mind wants to be free,
Why is it that the grim reaper is still out haunting me.

I know I walk around alive, but inside I feel so dead,
I put down the gun and slowly, reluctantly, slip into my bed.
I made it through another day, now it's time to say good-night,
So I just reach over and turn out the light.

PREMATURE DEATH

On the hill I heard a shot,
As I went down on one knee
With a hole in his chest
His eyes pleaded with me.

Yelled for a corpsman,
Ordered to advance up the hill again,
Passing over all the other wounded
And dead young men.

Moisture pouring down my face
Until the battle ends,
Then moved back down the hill,
I wanted to help my friend.

We gained nothing
And risked everything we had,
Saw them place my friend
Inside a body bag.

Another premature death,
Not a chance to return home--
Why do I always make it,
Only to be left standing all alone?

NAM WAS A CHESSBOARD

He's crossing the rice paddy
And I feel my eyes dilate.
With veins pumping I look down my barrel,
Through my sight,

Like a snake I slither,
Ahead just a foot or two
Slowly, I squeeze the trigger,
This is what I was sent to do.

The NVA are valueless,
Just an object, not even a man--
We're all valueless, used in this game,
The chessboard was Vietnam.

I see another pawn,
The fool moves too slow, he is just too late.
My rifle bucks into my shoulder,
"Checkmate."

SORROW

Take off my helmet,
Sit by his side.
He can't control the sorrow
For his friend that died.

I told him to chill out,
He must gain control.
They were now with God,
That's where all the combat vets go.

Told me he no longer wants friends,
Not as long as he was here.
Told him I knew the feeling,
As now, my eyes began to tear.

FREEDOM TO SING

Just a reminder, I want you to know,
There's stories to tell.
Who fought for your freedom
So you could march and yell?
"Hell no we won't go!"

Some say, "My country,"
Right or wrong--
They died so you could
Sing your song.
"Hell no we won't go!"

Some call us baby killers,
Some say we lost face
Yet we fought and died so you
Can march and yell all over the place.
"Hell no we won't go!"

You get to enjoy holidays,
Free to travel where ever you want to go.
We paid the price, so hold your head high,
Let your pride show. Next Memorial Day sing
"Hell no we won't go!"

Visit the 58,479 names
On the black granite "Wall," it won't take long.
They died so you could sing
And shout your song.
"Hell no we won't go!"

THE NIGHT

I can hardly see movement in the night
They make no sound, stay out of sight.
There is no sun, they are good all right,
Thank God, the moon is bright.

I see dark shadows move down the trail,
Still no sound, they do their job well.
Line them up in my sight,
It's hard to do in the middle of the night.

Clouds move overhead, feelings of doom,
There is no more light from the moon.
Now I see nothing, everything is black,
Someone yells, "Behind you Jack!"

I roll to my left, NVA standing over me,
Make out a shadow, but can hardly see.
What's this, a rotting body, he's already dead.
He still tries to kill me, I place four rounds in his head.

He falls to the ground, I jump to my feet,
Move back, look down, see blood and bits of meat.
A hand grabs my leg, his body has no head,
How in the hell do you kill someone that's dead?

I blow off his arm, then let out a scream
My girl shakes me, "what's wrong?" just a silly dream.

IT WILL HEAL

Vividly etched into the psyche of my mind,
The Vietnam war, a long time left behind.
Day or night, night or day
Always there, casting dark shadows in my way.

Night terror, nightmare,
My mind rips from all the wear.
It will heal, give it time,
Sand away, at what is etched in my mind.

It's only been twenty years, I can last twenty more.
After all, this wasn't even considered a war.
I survived, this war I had to play--
Get out the sand paper and sand it away.

Sure, it takes time to sand down the groove,
But it won't go away until I make my move.
Yes, it hurts, I know it takes time.
It must be done, if I want peace of mind.

PART V

REMEMBERING......
BROTHERS & SISTERS

THE WALL

I can't seem to find many words to say,
I flew to Washington DC, to face the wall today.
I must admit it's something I always knew I'd dread.
Guess I never wanted to admit, most my friends were dead.

I've avoided this trip over twenty years,
And now the past few days has had me in tears.
I guess this means there is still something inside alive,
God only knows this is the longest I have cried.

On panel fifteen E, line one hundred thirteen,
I found my first friend, a mighty fine Marine.
I hold the paper over his name,
Rub gently, as James T. Byrd appears in the frame.

All these names, a price to be free,
I gather my friends names to return home with me.
I wear my division colors to show who I was with in the war,
A young man asked if I knew his dad, he too was with the 3/4.

This took me totally by surprise,
And we both break down with tears in our eyes.
I fumble for some words, not knowing what to say.
God, I wish I'd known his dad to give some peace of mind today.

I pin my Marine Corps emblem and division colors on his shirt,
And tell him, "No, but son, I do know your pain and hurt
Wear your fathers colors while you're here today."
"If a Marine sees these colors, he will surely come your way."

I tell him his father would be proud, knowing he was here today
I hold him tight and said "Good luck son," he turns and walks away.
I hear a few guys laugh and cry, some even cuss
This part of the war's over for me, "Good-bye brothers," I head for the bus.

WHAT CAN I SAY

Howdy brothers,

What can I say?
I knew I'd have to face this Wall someday.
Sorry I didn't make it earlier-- I didn't have the guts.
Just the thought of facing this has driven me half nuts.

I'm still mixed-up, confused...
Was it really worth it, or were we just used?
It's kind of hard to stand tall
When we were spit on, and over 58,000 are on this Wall.

Readjustment has been hard after what we went through.
War, then spit, and rotten eggs, now standing before all of you.
The movies they put out are an absolute joke:
Drugs, drinking, and rape shoved down the viewers throats.

They have yet to make a movie about all of you
Jungle, fighting, death and dying for the good ole red, white and blue.
Well, brothers, what can I say?
This is all I can handle for today.

I'll be back tomorrow hopefully in a better mood,
Thinking about what you died for is giving me an attitude.

Later, Bro's--
"The Widow Maker"

THE CONFLICT

If ours was not a war,
What did over 58,000 men and women die for?

If it was not a war why did our country call,
Why are there over 58,000 names etched on the Wall?

If it was not a war, why did it last ten years,
Causing so much grief and so many tears?

If it was not a war,
What in the hell were we dying for?

OPERATION FREEDOM BIRD

It was a sad day in a good way,
As I stood wondering what to say,
Over 58,000 names before me, on the "Wall."
America West Airlines flew me there, so I could see it all.

It's part of a program done once a year,
Operation Freedom Bird is the reason I made it there.
Best Western Hotel, provided me with a place to stay--
Really strange for a Nam vet, to be treated that way.

For three days, I was their guest, in Washington DC.
It was overwhelming, red carpet treatment, given to me.
Many emotions went through my mind:
Sorrow, pain, hate, rage, it was an emotional time.

It was an experience, I needed to go through.
Just not at the top of my list, of things I wanted to do.
This was my first beginning of an end.
I moved along the Wall, from friend to friend.

I rubbed off names on paper provided to me,
Fought back tears, didn't let anyone see.
It was such a useless, insane war.
Even today, few can say, what it was really for.

A plane of combat nurses mixed with combat vets,
Made a great support team, I for one, have no regrets.
I had no idea, the nurses were under such strain.
I was glad they could open up to me, and share some pain.

The nurses memorial statue was dedicated today.
God, I hope this recognition helps their pain go away,
The Wall, a statue, something for everyone to touch,
A tribute to our brothers and sisters, really isn't asking much.

A place to grieve side by side, to honor those that have died --
Where once a year, we can feel some sense of pride.
The rest of the world would like to see us fade away,
Very little coverage done anymore on Veterans' Day.

People have no concept of the sacrifice
We the living still have to pay the price.
As long as time leaves one veteran out there,
I find peace in knowing one person will care.

America West Airlines, Best Western Hotel.
The only ones who care about us, that went through hell.
I can only offer them my utmost respect
Let them know their care and that trip, I shall never forget.

For me, you are the meaning of the red, white, and blue
You care for this nations veterans, and you follow through.

NURSES MEMORIAL STATUE

This was the year put to the test,
Flown to the Wall, courtesy of American West.
Face the fears, that have haunted me, for so long,
I was glad this was the first year combat nurses came along.

The nurse's memorial statue, to be placed this Veterans' Day,
Recognition for women who cared for us, when we got blown away.
There were a few with whom I did get the chance to talk,
Shared pain, checked out names, as in front of the Wall we walked.

Tears in her eyes, and tears in mine,
Shared the locked in sorrow, held in for such a long time.
It made me feel good, knowing the nurses wouldn't be slighted--
When it comes to Vietnam, everything is fast and one-sided.

In the parade we marched side by side,
Brothers and sisters, standing tall for once, feeling a bit of pride.
To all of you nurses who dealt with the pain, and made it through:
It was a proud moment for me, to be a part of you.

PART VI

YOU ARE NOT ALONE

YOUR JOURNEY BACK TO LIFE

All journey's begins with the first step. Any journey worth taking has a destination with provisions made for the anticipated emergency stops. If too much is left to chance, the result can be that the destination is never reached.

The purpose of this book is to serve as a guide for getting started on your own journey. A journey back to your life. All roads have potholes and the road to life is no exception. They can be navigated if you stay alert and prepare for your destination to rejoin the world. Everyone's journey will be different, but each individual is in charge of their own journey and must take responsibility.

You have taken the first step by reading these poems. Now take the second step: The first thoughts that come to your mind as you read--- take notes, write them down. The third step: Try writing poems of your own. They don't have to be polished; let your mind flow and write down the words, just as they come naturally. The fourth step: Share your writings with someone you care about. For the first time you may be able to express things you have kept inside, unable to talk about in normal conversation because finding the right words seemed impossible.

This is why writing is an important communication tool. What you just couldn't say, you'll find you can write. Sure, it's taking an enormous chance, but putting your thoughts on paper is part of you. If you feel it is important enough to show, it's important enough for that someone to know and you must start somewhere.

These poems encompass the Vietnam experience. I wrote down everything I saw and felt. First being drafted, next boot camp, then right into battle in Vietnam. I watched my friends die, become disfigured, dismembered; there was endless blood, grave rats, jungle rot, and nightmares. I lived in holes, ate from cans, killed, and thought about being killed.

I encourage you to write about your experience. It's time to let out those feelings you've been holding in for so long. Take a good look and be willing to share them with others. This wont be easy, but at least you will be able to see all the things inside of you that need to be dealt with. Knowing where the problems lie will put you ahead of many others who haven't quite figured out what to do. You have nothing to lose, and so much to gain.

HELPING YOURSELF

By reading this book, you have taken the first few steps in finding your way back. This is the beginning; you have come this far and there is no stopping you now. You may be stuck in the 60's or early 70's holding on to things you can't shake, even though you want to let go. I know from experience that you must go back and deal with what's blocking you. Then and only then, can you move forward into your life; your future.

These poems are similar to that probe a dentist uses to poke around recesses that haven't been touched. Like the probe, there will be those extremely tender, often painful places that make you come right out of your chair. No matter how dreadful, it must be done to prevent festering, inflammation, and infection. If left unattended, these little time bombs, (just waiting to go off), could result in a painful death.

Use these poems as a tool to go back into those deep, dark, hidden places in your mind, then you can begin to repair and heal. There will be pain involved; that is part of the healing process. You can easily endure this, since there is no comparison to the daily pain you've been living with by suppressing festering, unattended mental sores.

I relived my Vietnam experience by writing these poems and then showed them to a significant person in my life. It was the only way for me to express my feelings when I couldn't find the right words to say. There must be a significant person in your life you can go to first to share your writings with: a spouse, a friend, your doctor, your counselor or your rap group. After the initial breakthrough you may decide to continue on, letting the other people you trust read what you wrote. The important thing is that you "do" share what you've written with someone... someone significant.

Now you're saying, "This guy sounds like a really well adjusted social butterfly who made this happen easily." Not so! I had all the stereotypical markings of an "untouchable Vietnam vet." I had long hair and a beard to match. I wore an old field jacket and combat boots. I walked around with my knuckles dragging on the ground, in a fuzzy headed state of mind, maintained by drugs or booze or both with the disposition of an arthritic grizzly.

I believed the only thing anyone had to say to me was "move." I certainly didn't want nor did I even seem capable of saying the most common greeting. As an employee, I was the guy to steer clear of; one you better not cross, one you didn't count on to be around long enough to take advantage of any type of retirement plan. I'm the guy whose definition of major trauma would be: "dropping my cigarette and getting ashes on myself, or spilling my coffee while reaching for the cream." You could count on me to rearrange the furniture and change the contour of the house, and at the same time bring the neighbors out of a dead sleep. Recognize Me?

I'm not that guy anymore. Believe me, it wasn't easy to get to this point. It took years. Don't let that sound discouraging because it took years to get as screwed up as I was. The cure should take at least as much time.

There are several things you can get out of sharing those dark areas....your secrets that the probe digs out---release, rediscovery of trust, networking, and achieving goals:

RELEASE---You go back and take a look at what you saw, what you did, and how you felt. Once you admit it to someone, the pressure is off because you no longer are the keeper of the secret. That is *release!*

TRUST---When you took that seemingly larger-than-life chance by showing your secrets to someone, you *trusted* their reaction. Each time we trust, (and amazingly enough), aren't let down or disappointed in that trust, we feel free to trust again. Old feelings start to return, possibly ones you haven't felt since Vietnam....and it feels good!

NETWORKING---This is one of the most important steps on your journey back. It is only possible after you have learned to trust again. Say to yourself, "Of all the patrols I went on, I didn't go alone. I had help then and I need help now." A rap group, a vet counselor or a Vietnam vet organization is a great place to start. When I started sharing my writing with people, eventually they became members of my rap group. There were times when I was struggling with this and needed to touch base with my rap group almost desperately. I would drive 240 miles a week at times just to be in that group. It's important to feel safe in the group you choose. Give it more than one chance. If it doesn't feel right to you after that, find another group or organization. It's going to be an important factor. There are no real reasons for not going....only excuses.

GOALS---The first goal I set was to accept myself (anything after that feat came pretty easy). I found out by sharing, then trusting, then networking that I had to make some changes. I realized that I was the only one who could make these changes. Why? Because like it or not, fair or unfair, the world is not going to change for you or me. That's okay because that puts the right person in charge...yourself. The goal of accepting yourself is a daily task, but will be part of every other goal you set.

When setting goals, make sure that you set goals you can realistically meet. You're going to need that feeling of success to keep you motivated for the next goal. Since I didn't smile or talk to anyone (I didn't have to for such a long time) that was one of my first goals. It was my way of saying "World I'm coming back!" I wasn't sure the facial muscles were up to the task so I practiced in the mirror first. I stood there with a crooked mouth and managed to evince the word, "Hi!"

In the beginning my smiles were "forced." Those early smiles I laid on people and the word "Hi," coming from between my nearly clenched teeth must have taken some of them back. They stared or said nothing at all. I thought "To hell with that experiment!" Then I reminded myself that they couldn't know what my smile and "Hi" meant. It was just as new to me as it was to them. I was persistent and after about a month I started to get positive response. I was gaining ground and having success! I rolled along saying "Hi!" and smiling.....piece of cake.

Then people began wanting to have conversation with me. It took me by surprise. I had neither prepared nor practiced for this occurrence. This was unfamiliar territory to me. I had not used any conversational skills in over 17 years. I had to fall back, retreat and set a 360 around me. Fortunately, in all the years I didn't talk to people I spent time reading. I read that the best conversationalist is the one who will listen. Who is a better listener that a Vietnam vet? Vietnam vet's aren't used to talking much so listening should be easy.

That retreat came as a result of not being prepared. Of all the experiences in Vietnam, something of a positive and useful nature should come to mind....being prepared. We didn't go on patrol or out on an operation without being fully prepared. We blackened our faces, loaded up heavily on everything we needed, taped our dog tags, etc. We left little, if anything, to chance. Why then was I going out into the world unprepared? With no plans for the unexpected or even the expected?

Another skill I learned in Vietnam applied to daily living. Prepare for only one day at a time. Our total concentration was set on that one operation. Not yesterday or tomorrow, just today. That's how I prepare and set my goals now. I prepare for today. Yesterday is history....something to learn from, not dwell on. Tomorrow is tomorrow and will be here soon enough.

Once I was able to get back into the habit of conversation the importance of networking came into play. I needed and wanted a job. I was no longer satisfied with my work record as it stood. I told someone I trusted that I was looking for work in earnest. I found a horrible job but I stuck to it. I worked hard until I could find something better. Brothers and sisters who knew me from rap groups and vet organizations were willing to give me recommendations. They knew where a guy like me might be able to get a toe in.

By then, I was open to personal suggestions; (before, such suggestions would have sent me on my way). I cleaned up and dressed for the world I was ready to join and I did it without compromising who I am. I dress appropriately for work but when I'm on my own time, I am free to dress as expressively as I want, and I do.

I knew if I was going to get a better job I would have to learn some self-control skills. I couldn't let down the brothers and sisters who stood up for me and recommended me for the job. I had to find a new way to deal with my anger and frustration of daily living. Something I hadn't had much success with.

Everyone has different ways to relax, and you can find what works for you. I consciously tell a certain part of my body to relax and concentrate on relaxing that specific spot until it happens. It was so simple. I was almost ashamed I didn't think of it sooner. Once I learned to relax I learned to control myself, my rage. I learned that anger can't be vented any time and place, but can be vented later and constructively.

Something to try:

1. Get a punching bag and name it the frustration or person giving you a hard time. You need to get your anger and frustration out of your system; and this is a way to do it without losing your job or landing in jail.

2. Find a disciplined form of physical exercise. I chose karate and soon became an instructor.

3. Write out your frustrations. I've sent guys to hell with some of the letters I've written. I never mailed them, but just having a pen in my hand and getting it from my head to the paper takes care of the problem and gets me through one more day. I seldom have to resort to this anymore. I start each day prepared. I've got a grip on myself and am in better control.

I try to anticipate if a situation or a person could set me off and if at all possible, I get out of there. Confrontations over every little annoyance aren't necessary and completely avoidable. The more control I acquired, the more confident I became. I was able to use my networking abilities to move up the ladder of better job offers with each step. It took tenacity, but I hung in there. I worked seven months shoveling rock.

A Nam vet (networking) helped get me off the pile and on to a better job. He told me how to go about it, so I let personnel know daily I was around and I was interested in a job. Finally they gave me a chance to work part time; then it turned into a full time job. I take one day at a time and I stay prepared.

There are a lot of Nam vets out there making a comeback. They can help anyone who wants to help themselves. You have to break your world of suffering and make contact with them, as I did. In the bush when you were pinned down, there wasn't anything you could do about it. When the rockets, mortars, and artillery were pouring in all you could do was stay in your hole and pray. There is nothing pinning you down now, there is no reason to remain in your hole. Your new challenge, your new high...is change. You already know how to fight for every inch of ground; you already know that falling back is not retreating. You already know that each day you succeed brings you closer to home but home this time is release from your suffering and some peace of mind.

I had always been upset with my family for not understanding me, yet I was the one who never told them things. Then I let them read my book. They said they had no idea this is how it was in Nam. I just let them read on and now we talk about things slowly. After 17 years they were ready to ask questions and finally I was ready to answer.

Three weeks after my return from Vietnam, I was asked to leave home. I was not the fun-loving guy they use to known. I was a combat vet who talked little and yelled a lot. I stayed drunk and used drugs. I don't blame my parents for asking me to leave. We never talked and now the book explained so much. They finally understand what I went through and I understand what I put them through because they didn't know how to talk to me. They didn't say, "Poor Jack, we didn't know." They just accepted me for who I am now and said, "We have a much better understanding and if you ever want to talk, we are here." There was a time when they feared me but now they show me the care that was always there and that is all I ever wanted from them.

It is my fervent hope and prayer that this book in some way helps those who read it.

Jack D. Adams

COMBAT HISTORY
JACK D, ADAMS VIETNAM 1966-1967
DETAILS

Major Operations in Vietnam that accounted for more that 500 known NVA and Viet Cong killed. These were considered some of the most bloody operations of the war. They can be found in most combat history books.

Operation Prairie lasted 182 days.
August 3rd of 1966 through January of 1967. This was a continuing 3rd Marine Division operation, which fought the NVA along the Demilitarized Zone. We fought against well trained NVA troops of 324th -B Division. There were 1,397 known enemy casualties.

Operation Prairie-II lasted 46 days.
This was a continuation of the 3rd Marine Division operations along the area of the DMZ. There were 893 known enemy casualties.

Operation Buffalo lasted 13 days.
This was also a continuation of 3rd Marine Division operations along the DMZ and were followed by Operations *Cimarron* and *Hickory* which accounted for 1,201 known enemy casualties.

Operation *Kingfisher - Hickory-II - Kentucky* and *Lancaster* lasted 108 days. This was also a continuation of 3rd Marine Division operations. These operations accounted for 1,117 enemy casualties.

Other Operations and duties I performed were:

Participated in the defense of *Dong Ha- Quang Tri.* Province against the Communist Viet Cong in South Vietnam.

Participated in the defense of *Cam Lo Quang Tri.* Province against the Communist Viet Cong.

Participated in *Operation Prairie-III*.

Participated in Operation Prairie-IV. During this battle, I was wounded on May 30th 1967 receiving an enemy NVA grenade blast which blinded me and received fragment wounds to the face and body. I was out of action for a few weeks.

Participated in *Operation Hickory-III*.

These were the operations. This doesn't account for the many search and destroy missions, the day patrols, or night ambushes in which contact was made and the enemy as well as our own were killed. I wrote to Headquarters Marine Corps requesting my After Action Combat Report, along with my Operations reports. They sent me as much as they could in all area's.

I wanted to put all of these pages in this book, but these were copies sent to me and they would be unreadable if reduced down to fit on these pages.

Had I been able to do this, you could have read where they were stamped *Secret*, and some stamped *Unclassified* since enough time has passed. You could have read about the fire support missions we received from many bases with Artillery Support, Air Support and Naval Fire Support and so much more.

This is the best I can offer for the Action and Operations I was a part of.

GLOSSARY

AK-47 Russian made Kalashnikov automatic rifle, gas operated, magazine-fed, air cooled, full and semi-automatic weapon firing a 7.62 cartridge. Magazine holds 30 rounds with an effective range of 400 meters. Standard rifle of the North Vietnamese Army.

AGENT ORANGE A toxin used as a defoliant in Vietnam.

ARTILLERY ROUND Larger caliber than machine guns ammunition. Used in mounted guns. Classified according to caliber's: light, medium, or heavy.

ARVN Army of the Republic of Vietnam (South Vietnam).

B 52 Boeing Stratofortress, United States Air Force. Eight engine, swept wing, heavy jet bomber. Used in Vietnam for strikes against area targets such as troop concentrations and base areas. Carried 84 bombs, 750 pounds.

BAMBOO POLES The trunk of a bamboo shoot or tree.

BAMBOO ROOF A thatched roof made from bamboo poles and leaves.

BAMBOO VIPER A small poisonous snake commonly referred in Vietnam as a one-step or two-step. (How many steps the bitten victim takes before the poison is lethal).

BASE OF FIRE Men firing machine guns; providing a cover for advancing troops to find positions for combat.

BEETLE NUTS A food staple found throughout Vietnam's jungles, used by Vietnamese population as a quick food.

BLACK POT A cauldron used for cooking over open fires.

BN Battalion.

BOOBY TRAP A concealed mechanism designed to operate and cause damage when inadvertently disturbed, specifically a bomb, mine, etc.. It is actuated by casual or careless movements of the enemy.

BOOT CAMP The primary training station for enlisted military personnel. (Because of the leggins or boots worn by the recruits).

BRASS CASINGS Encases part of the bullet holding the lead propellant and the gun powder.

BREAD CAN One of the small cans in the C- ration packs, holding the bread stuff.

BUNKER A steel or concrete fortification usually underground. In Vietnam these were fortified with sand bags, (A bulwark of earth erected to protect a gun emplacement).

BUSH Refers to the jungle in Vietnam.

C-130 Lockheed Hercules. A four engine turboprop transport aircraft.

CAMMIES (BDU) Battle Dress Uniform. Camouflaged fatigues.

CANTEEN A small metal or plastic flask for drinking water.

CHARLIE Refers to the communist Vietnamese soldier.

CHOPPER Slang for helicopter.

CLAYMORE A mine with a curved block of explosives containing steel pellets on the convex side. Set above ground with the side of pellets facing the enemy. Commonly used in ambushes, night defenses and perimeters. Command detonated.

CLIP An appliance that clasps, grips or holds fast a metal container holding cartridges for rapid-fire gun, as an automatic rifle.

COMBAT VET One who served in the armed forces referring to one who has been in action or fighting with the enemy.

CONG Refers to enemy Vietnamese military man.

CORPSMAN A member of the military corps. An enlisted man working as a medical technician assigned to a specific combat area.

GLOSSARY ★ 153

CP Command Post.

C-RATIONS Combat rations. Small cans of all the food groups. They are about the size of tuna fish cans.

DOG TAGS A pendant or small metal plate. A soldiers identification tag worn around the neck on a chain.

DMZ Demilitarized Zone. The line separating North and South Vietnam.

DOOR GUNNER A guardian of keeper of a helicopter door. He sits by the back door manning a machine gun to provide cover for on-loading and off-loading troops.

DUNG Refers to human waste products such as urine and feces.

E TOOL Excavation tool. A small shovel that folds to make more potable.

FATIGUES Sturdy work clothing worn by soldiers doing fatigue duty.

FLACK JACKET Muti-layered jacket of fatigue material used as a bulletproof vest.

FLASHBACKS A break in continuity made by the presentation of an episode of event occurring earlier. It effects the senses such as seeing, smelling, tasting and feeling the event.

FRIENDLY FIRE Shot at or fired upon by your own forces.

FRONT LINE In Vietnam no established lines. Refers to making direct contact with the enemy at any point in the jungle.

GOOK Refers to anyone of oriental descent.

GRENADE A small bomb designed to be thrown by hand or fired from a rifle or launching device exploding on impact or by action of a time fuse.

GRENADE LAUNCHER M-79 made in the United States. Single shot, breech-loaded shoulder weapon which fires 40mm projectiles and weighs approximately 6.5 pounds when loaded. It has a sustained rate of fire of five-seven rounds per minute and an effective range of 375 meters.

GRUNT Slang for rifleman or infantryman. The foot soldier.

HEAT TAB A small tablet carried in the C-Ration pack of compressed fuel burning for three to five minutes after ignition.

HOOCH Slang for a small one man tent.

HUEY Popular name for UH-1 series of helicopters.

HUMP Walking through the jungle in full combat gear.

HUTS Bamboo houses used for shelter by the Vietnamese people.

INCOMING This word was yelled when enemy mortar, artillery, or rocket-fire began to fall in your position.

JUNGLE ROT Refers to an infection of any opening in the skin such as cuts, bug bites or wounds.

K-BAR A fighting knife.

KIA Killed In Action.

LAW M-72 anti-tank weapon. Light weight and fired one time only using a 66mm rocket to destroy bunkers or enemy troops.

LISTENING POST Six to eight man hole in front of established perimeters to monitor enemy advancing activity; usually by radio.

LZ Landing Zone. Area used to pick up or drop off troops.

MACHINE GUN M-60 Made in the United States, belt fed, gas-operated, air coiled, 7.62mm automatic weapon. Weighs approximately twenty pounds without mount or ammunition. It has a sustained rate of fire of one hundred rounds per minute and an effective range of a thousand meters.

MAGAZINE A receptacle in which the supply of reserve cartridges is placed.

MARINE A soldier trained for service at sea and on land. A member of the Marine Corps, a branch of the United States Navy made up of combat troops, under their own officers. The oldest organized military or naval body in the United States. Officially authorized in 1775.

MIA Missing In Action.

MOS A number assigned to men. *i.e.* 0311--means rifleman.

M-79 "The bloop tube," (for the sound it made when fired). A stubby, short barreled M-406 grenade launcher; resembling a single shot break-open sawed off shot gun. Highly accurate within two hundred meters in the hand of and experienced operator. First used by the U.S. Army in 1961,

NAPALM A bomb containing a jell substance that burns.

NIGHT AMBUSH Squad of six to eight men under-cover at night. Sent to known enemy locations to engage in combat.

NVA North Vietnamese Army. A foot mobile army of men; the regular force of the Hanoi government.

OUT HOUSE Latrine or shelter for toileting purposes.

OVERRUN Large numbers of enemy troops breaking through parameters.

PACK Fatigue canvas bag used to carry supplies worn by soldiers on patrol.
i.e. extra pair of socks, c-rat's, medical supplies, and extra ammo.

PUNGI PIT Small holes dug in the ground containing sharpened bamboo spikes smeared with human feces or poisons to cause infection when the skin is punctured. Concealed along trails covered with bamboo and leaves.

RIFLE M-14 Gas operated, magazine fed, air-coiled, semi-automatic, 7.62mm caliber shoulder weapon. It weighs twelve pounds with a full 20-round magazine, sustained rate of fire: 30 rounds per minute. Effective range: 460 meters.

RIFLE M-16 Gas operated, magazine fed, air-coiled, automatic, 5.56mm caliber shoulder weapon. It weighs 3.1 pounds with a 20-round magazine, sustained rate of fire: 12-15 rounds per minute. Effective range: 460 meters.

RVN Republic of Vietnam; (South Vietnam).

7.62 The size of an ammo round used in the M-14 and M-16 rifles.

782 GEAR Gear used in combat.

SHORT TIMER In country troop with less than thirty days left on tour of duty.

SMOKE GRENADE Hand thrown bomb containing colored smoke to alert choppers of locations. Red means enemy present; green means clear to land.

SPIDER HOLE Viet Cong guerrilla one-man hole; dug in the ground with a cover camouflaged to match the terrain. Used to ambush enemy troops and sometimes connected to the tunnel complex.

TANK M 48 Built in the United States. A 50.7 ton tank with a crew of four men. Primary armament is turret-mounted 90mm gun; uses one .30 caliber and one .50 caliber machine gun. Maximum road speed: 32mph. Average range: 195 miles.

TUNNEL RAT Slang used for the smaller men that searched the tunnel network in the jungle, carrying a .45 and a flashlight.

USA United States Army.

USAF United States Air Force.

USMC United States Marine Corps.

USN United States Navy.

VC Viet Cong. Communist military troops consisting of guerrilla squads and platoons.

VIET MINH Vietnamese contraction for Viet Nam Doc Lap Nong Minh Hoi. A communist-led coalition of nationalist groups which actively opposed the Japanese in WWII and the French in the first Indochina War.

VET Short for veteran.

VETERAN One who served in the armed forces.

WIA Wounded in Action.

ABOUT THE AUTHOR

Born in Chunte, Kansas, and raised in California, he joined the United States Marine Corps in 1966. After completing boot camp training at Camp Pendleton, San Diego, he was assigned to Third Battalion, Forth Marines, Third Marine Division, and choppered into the jungle to join his new outfit in Operation Hastings. He fought in Operation Prairie, Prairie II, Prairie III. On May 30th (Memorial Day), 1967, during Operation Prairie IV, he was wounded in combat trying to take hill 484. General Bruno A. Hochmuth pinned the Purple Heart on him during his recovery at the hospital in Phu Bai (only a few weeks later the General's helicopter was shot down, killing the General and all crew members on board). After a quick recovery he was sent back to the jungle and fought in the following operations: Hickory, Cimarron, Buffalo, Hickory II, Kingfisher, and Hickory III. These battles can be found in the Marine Corps history books and are referred to as some to the bloodiest of the war. By the end of his tour over five thousand enemy were killed in the operations in which he was involved. Due to his small stature, he was utilized as a "tunnel rat" to explore enemy holes along the DMZ. His tangible assets were the standard Marine Corps rack of ribbons and medals plus a few extra for deeds done. His awards include: The Purple Heart, Presidential Unit Citation for Extraordinary Heroism, Vietnam Meritorious Unit Citation for Heroism, Vietnam Cross of Gallantry, Combat Action Ribbon, Vietnam Campaign Medal, Vietnam Service Medal with Star, and National Defense Medal.

Mental suffering, more often than not, manifests itself in the dreams of the nightmare variety. The nightmare visions start spilling over into the days, severely hampering the best efforts to cope with even minimal day-to-day activity. In an effort to dispel the crippling effect of these dreams, he started to write down his dreams and thoughts and it helped. He wrote seemingly unmentionable things onto paper. Things he never could have verbalized, even to the therapist. Next he took a real chance and let someone read them. For the first time there was communication.

Adams continually works to keep his promise. "All who served and sacrificed will not be forgotten." He was an instrumental part of chartering chapters of the Military Order of the Purple Heart and Vietnam Veterans of America. He served as Commander of the Military Order of the Purple Heart and three-year Director for the Military Order of the Purple Heart #608, Arizona's State Legislative Officer for the Military Order of the Purple Heart, three-year Director of Vietnam Veterans of America second Vice President Vietnam Veterans of America, Legislative Officer for Disabled American Veterans, and State Representative for WIMSA, (Women In Military Service to America). He has received Citations and awards from: The Military Order of the Purple Heart, Veterans of Foreign Wars, Disabled American Veterans, National League of Families and American Prisoners of Missing in Southeast Asia, the All Veteran Memorial Statue, and many more.

He was involved in a variety of successful projects such as the Outreach Vet Center, a nursing home for veterans, and the Veterans Memorial Statue were all built in Prescott, Arizona. He posed for the statue's wounded soldier located on the courthouse plaza.

He has written over 1,200 letters to Dignitaries and Celebrities, receiving over 400 caring responses from the White House, the Senate, Congress, actors, actresses, singers and sport teams. He framed and arranged these autographed pictures and letters to create a *Tribute to Veterans' Display*. It is a speaking memorial for all Americans to view and enjoy, in honor of all veterans, and will continue to grow.

He is the Military and Veteran Liaison for TCWR records. "A musical milestone." Featuring fourteen original songs written in recognition and honor of the American Veteran. The same statue he posed for in Prescott, Arizona, was used to grace the cover of this "Veteran Tribute" album. He appeared on a TNN special hour of *Prime Time Country* with B.J. Thomas, Johnny PayCheck, Freddie Hart, and Craig Harris, in honor of the album and all veterans.

Because of Jack's continuous dedication and self sacrifice, there is now a chance to bring all who served and all who were lost into the new millennium. They will not be forgotten. He is co-founder of "TAPS," *The American Patriotic Site*, an ongoing project that will encompass 820 acres and become America's largest Patriotic Center. TAPS will not only be a place for everyone to enjoy and reflect back, but an educational experience that could possibly bring back lost patriotism and feelings of pride. TAPS will honor all who served, fought, bled and died for America. A monumental reminder of the price we paid for our freedom and a way to preserve our military history.

Adams resides in Carthage, Tennessee, with his dog Zion.